STOP
He Will Find You
T. Dailey

A Personal Testimony of Bondage and Deliverance Part 1

Copyright © 2018 Tonya M. White Dailey

All rights reserved. No part of this publication may be reproduced, distributed, or transmitted in any form or by any means, including photocopying, recording, or other electronic or mechanical methods, without the prior written permission of the publisher, except in the case of brief quotations embodied in critical reviews and certain other noncommercial uses permitted by copyright law.

ISBN-13: 978-1-970079-50-0

Published by Opportune Independent Publishing Company

For permission requests, write to the publisher, addressed "Attention: Permissions Coordinator" to the address below.

Email: Info@opportunepublishing.com

Address: 113 N. Live Oak Street
Houston, TX 77003

My Personal Diary Part 1

"...there is more joy in heaven over one lost sinner who repents and returns to God than over ninety-nine others who are righteous and haven't strayed away!"

—Luke 15:7, NLT

Table of Contents

DEDICATION		8
PURPOSE		9
SPECIAL THANKS		11
INTRODUCTION		13
CHAPTER 1	While Searching for God, Fear Got Me	21
CHAPTER 2	Doubt and the Great Divide	31
CHAPTER 3	Lies and Promises Were Lookin' Good	37
CHAPTER 4	Did You Mean to Destroy My Life?	57
CHAPTER 5	This is Killing Me	91
CHAPTER 6	Summary	129

Dedication

This book is dedicated to my three children, and any mother who ever wished she could do things over again.

Purpose

I'm writing to the Christian mothers who are raising their children in the fear of the Lord. I hope you stop your busy schedule and read this with open hearts. This is a message from one Christian mother to another. My testimony happened after I joined a small church in Germany several years ago. I am both ashamed and embarrassed at how I spent the next twenty years doing my own thing, living in sin, all while I praised God on Sundays. I was lukewarm in my Christian walk and ended up facing something that I almost did not escape!

The purpose of this book is two-fold. It is written to make you aware that there is something called spiritual abuse and it is more common than you think, happening right under our noses. And secondly, Jesus, the son of God and true Messiah, is here to deliver us all if we let him.

To make things clear, I have included excerpts of my personal journal which are based on actual events. I was not aware of what was happening to me when everything began, but now I know for sure that I encountered a world of darkness and torment by satanic witchcraft. I believe that some of you are also battling the effects of witchcraft and other satanic attacks in your own lives, but most of you are not aware of it.

As members of God's army, it's time that we rise up against evil so that our families, loved ones and our own lives are really changed through complete biblical deliverance and healing. The Bible teaches that in taking a stand against evil, God will fight for us, through us, and with us.

Ephesians chapter 6 says this…

[10] Finally, be strong in the Lord and in his mighty power. [11] Put on the full armor of God, so that you can take your stand against the devil's schemes. [12] For our struggle is not against flesh and blood, but against the rulers, against the authorities, against the powers of this dark world and against the spiritual forces of evil in the heavenly realms. [13] Therefore put on the full armor of God, so that when the day of evil comes, you may be able to stand your ground, and after you have done everything, to stand. [14] Stand firm then, with the belt of truth buckled around your waist, with the breastplate of righteousness in place, [15] and with your feet fitted with the readiness that comes from the gospel of peace. [16] In addition to all this, take up the shield of faith, with which you can extinguish all the flaming arrows of the evil one. [17] Take the helmet of salvation and the sword of the Spirit, which is the word of God.

[18] And pray in the Spirit on all occasions with all kinds of prayers and requests. (New International Version)

Special Thanks

First, I thank Jesus Christ, the only true savior and my savior.

There are so many people that I'm thankful for, and unfortunately, I won't be able to list all of their names here. To all the prayer warriors I met along the way, my personal healing minister and church family, thank you so much for praying for me! I'm glad that your names are written in the book of life.

I thank God for my mom, sisters, and my whole biological family who had crazy prayer and determination to see my deliverance, and for my husband and mother-in-law for standing in the gap for so many years.

And it is with tears in my eyes that I am most grateful to God for my children: Letiza, Nathan and Daniel. As children, they had to helplessly watch the physical and psychological abuse, disillusionment and consequences of my decisions. No child should have had to endure what they did.

As I look back now, however, I believe that through it all, God chiseled out, in my children, who are now adults, great spiritual warriors for His kingdom.

Finally, I give special thanks to my publisher, editors, book designer and to all of those who made this book come alive. And I'm especially grateful for my best friend Debra who kept me grounded as I wrote this difficult testimony.

May Christ (the anointed Messiah of God) bless you all!

Introduction

Thirty years ago, I was an adulterer. I'm not proud of that. According to the Bible, being an adulterer is one of the most detestable sins. It was and still is an abomination to the Lord, and yet it seems that nowadays it is the thing to do, whether you are a Christian or not. It seems there's a sense that we are entitled to have what we want and who we want when we want it. If our spouses are not giving us what we want, we tend to give up on the relationship as if marriage is only based on a piece of paper.

When you are a Christian, marriage is not just a piece of paper, nor is it simply a ceremony or party filled with music and poetic vows.

In the sight of God, marriage is a bond between you, your groom, and God. That bond is more than words. It's made up of vows to God which means that God gets to have a say as to how things go. Marriage was originally God-made, not man-made. The first illustration of a marriage from God appears in Genesis chapter 1.

In the Scripture, God presented Eve to her husband which means that she was handpicked for him by God. These days, men and women are doing the picking and expecting God to get on board with our choices. Instead of seeking God for what he wants for our lives, it seems like God has to get on our schedule; God has to get with our plans and dreams.

In essence, we are creating God into our own image. And if we do get around to doing God's will, there are conditions to our commitment to Him. We seem to do God's will as long as it is under our guidelines. In other words, we will surrender to Him only to a certain point.

For a great number of Christians, we operate as if we are our own gods and we use God's name to help us accomplish our own goals. I know this to be true because that's the way I lived for nearly 25 years, and the evidence in our society suggests that I'm not alone.

We are living in a world that sees God as a means to get what we want. Some of us use education to get what we want, others use networking, but a vast number of us use God to get the things we desire. Most of us are waiting for God to bless us with our houses, our jobs, our buildings, our land, and the spouses that we want. For many, He is nothing more than a tool to gain more stuff. I know this is not the case for all, but I'm talking about a very large number of people, and it doesn't matter your social-economic background, nationality, race or gender; we have forgotten how to submit to a power greater than ourselves. Look around you. The condition of our society tells it all. We are our own gods!

The Bible teaches us that we all have fallen short of the glory of God (Romans 3:23), and many are still doing it while making excuses about it. We think we can continue to make excuses for our sins and still serve God without consequences. It's just not true that we can live in sin and expect God to tolerate it. God hates sin, and sin carries consequences. And yes, God is a loving God, but He still hates sin!

Despite our disobedience, God makes some very awesome promises to us as a people in His word, and there are many personal blessings that He has for us as well. The earth belongs to Him and it's His will to be gracious to us. Because of this, we know that there's nothing wrong with obtaining blessings, except for one thing. We have to be in God's will to receive particular blessings. Everyone enjoys the benefits of God's goodness whether they acknowledge Him in their lives or not.

God makes his sun to rise on the evil and on the good, on the just and unjust (Matthew 5:45). However, there are specific blessings that are promised to us that are only released through our obedience to Him. God has a will for His church and He has a will for each of us individually. He even has a specific will for our families as well.

God has both blessings and assignments for us, but in order to receive these things, we must come in line with His plan. And that requires us to submit to HIM and only Him. To *submit*, which is "hupotasso" in the Greek language, means to be under obedience; to be subordinate; to obey. (James 4:7) We cannot live our lives being our own bosses. That just doesn't work in the Kingdom of God.

Those are some hard words to swallow, and I suspect that today, more than ever, people are struggling with whether it's really necessary to give up their will to something that may or may not even be real.

It's apparent that the world seems to be struggling with the question: "Is God real or not?" Even people who claim to be Christian struggle from time to time as to whether God is real. From the looks of things, it seems that most folks have concluded that God is not real. And if he is real, it's only during our times of crisis. After the emergency is over, it's business as usual. Most of us live our lives believing in God when it is convenient. Maybe you're thinking that I've got it wrong and these things do not pertain to you. You may think that I must be talking about myself. Well, if you're thinking that, you're right. Everything I just explained above was me. I lived my life thinking I was serving God, but I came to realize that I was simply serving my own sinful ambition. The truth of that fact is what set me free. So, if you are like I was, this book is for you. If all of this is not you, then praise God!

More importantly, this book is also for anyone who is struggling with the question of whether God is alive. Let me first say that God is very much alive, and I believe my testimony will help you see that as well. If it were not for God literally showing up in my life, this book would NOT have been written.

A Snapshot of My Story

Based on what seemed to be a little decision I made at the age of 19 years old, my life took a sudden spin into a horrible nightmare where I ended up enduring physical, psychological, emotional, and spiritual abuse for nearly 28 years. In this lifestyle, I became a person that I never knew I could be, someone who was emotionally numb, full of pride and self-righteousness.

As unimaginable events began to unfold, I ran away from my husband who eventually divorced me after only three years of marriage. From my perspective, I was a Christian mother raising my three children in a holiness, Pentecostal church, but my husband saw something else.

I couldn't see the danger I was in even though my family tried to warn me. In general, I spent most of my years defending my decision to leave my husband and stay with my church.

I have to admit, now, that while I understood the many rules that I had to follow as a Christian, oftentimes I was sad at the way my life was. It was very restricted and seemed to be micromanaged, however, I still kept following the rules and obeying the pastor with complete loyalty, even in the face of strange decisions he made that caused me to question things from time to time.

For example, why was it so important that I wore dresses and skirts everywhere to show I was a Christian? I thought fruit of the holy spirit was the true evidence of salvation, not my clothes. Also, why were so many families who were a part of this church escaping in the middle of the night? Whenever another family left, I remember being told that everyone who left the pastor was somehow out of the will of God and they were enemies with the church. This and other things seemed to be a little questionable, but I was willing to hold on to our traditions despite my inner struggle to sometimes hold on to my beliefs.

As I write this book, I can't help but reflect on the people on the outside of the church who found our pastor and church to be abusive. At the time I was with the church, I never considered it abusive. I really couldn't put my finger on how to describe my church, other than just "different."

We were a family. I believed that for a long time, but those outside the church did not believe that we were simply a place of worship. After some years, they described our church as an abusive environment and several investigations began against the church. "Where was this coming from?," I thought to myself.

Despite allegations, I still held on to the notion that our church and pastor were not guilty of any criminal wrongdoings. Little did I know that my life would change forever based on my decision to support my church. Although wrestling privately with some of our traditions, I was convinced that my church was a safe place to raise my children under the fear of the Lord. I lived under this belief for many years until one day everything came crashing down.

The Department of Children's Services came in and removed my three children based on accusations of a crime that supposedly occurred in my church.

I remember thinking to myself, "Crime? What crime?" No words could describe the shame and embarrassment I felt and still feel at times. Has my whole life been a lie? This was too much to bear.

When this happened, nothing was real to me anymore. The world seemed empty and to live each day was purposeless. Not only was the church accused of allowing abuse, I was accused of allowing my children to be abused. I couldn't believe it. My body was numb, my emotions were raging. I couldn't understand why God let this happen to me.

Now, as I reflect on the events that led to my shame, it seemed like I was a prisoner in a jail with no walls, alone and fighting for my life, fighting for my true identity. It was hard to know who I had become. I had become a monster and couldn't recognize who was looking back at me in the mirror. You see, unknowingly, I had come to realize that I was living in a religious cult. It was a cult that worshipped man more than God.

Everyone else outside of the church who loved me could see it, but I couldn't because I had eyes but could not see and ears but could not hear. The only thing my biological family could do was to stand by helplessly and watch as my life slowly and methodically came unraveled. Years went by.

Suddenly one day, finding myself alone, homeless, psychologically and emotionally burned out, I finally cried out to Jesus with the loudest and deepest cry I could muster, and he found me. Some may say that God always knew where I was so He didn't have to find me. He knew all the time where I was; He knows everything. That's true, but there's something more to consider.

"Stop, He Will Find You," means something more than God simply searching for my whereabouts. No! He literally pursued me until I realized that I was lost. You see, you can be driving for so long on a road that looks familiar and actually be going in the wrong direction. That has happened to me a number of times while driving along the highway in another city on vacation. Let me tell you, it's a nightmare trying to get back on the right road. If it were not for someone guiding me, I would still be lost on that highway. That's how God found me some years ago - going down a highway in my life that was leading to a dead end. And I was not aware of it.

He found me in self-denial, self-deception, self-righteousness, and totally tangled-up in a web of confusion and emotional numbness. I was not pretty to look at, and in God's sight I smelled of sin and hypocrisy; but eventually I stopped trying to live my life like everything was ok. It wasn't ok. I stopped making excuses about the bad decisions I was making, and I stopped fighting against the truth.

Because of the mess I was in, I was not where I was supposed to be in God. I was utterly out of the place that God ordained for me. Just like God called Adam in the garden of Eden, He asked, "Where are you?" The question was rhetorical but very powerful. The answer to that question was not for God, but rather for Adam. It was a question that Adam was to reflect on. Adam used to be in the presence of God, but now he was in sin. God asked me that question too one day, "Where are you?" And I kept telling Him that everything was good until after some time, I stopped and really took a look at my life. I was lost! Really lost!

Everything was not good. You see, because He is omniscient, God knew exactly where I was in my life, but that did nothing for me until I actually realized it for myself. When I realized that I was lost, I stopped and asked for help. That's when God came into my life like a roaring ocean.

God saw the parts of me that I didn't see, and when I was aware of that, then that's when I was found. He looked past the shame, guilt, and the sin I had and found the person I was meant to be. He found that person in me and rescued her from hypocrisy, lies, self-deception, confusion and internal trauma.

And He rescued me in the most magnificent way, putting me in my right mind. I am still in awe to this day. Tears well up in my eyes as I move past this part of the writing. It's hard to believe that several years ago, I was actually lost in pride and self-deception so badly that no one could bring me out. Believe me, I was not coming out because I did not know that I was deceived until it was almost too late. How I was rescued still amazes me. From this, I learned that Jesus is the only true God.

Surprisingly, when Jesus responded to my cries, things didn't go the way I expected. I expected that all the problems I experienced would be fixed and that our church would heal and be thriving in the community. That did not happen. The opposite happened.

When the Lord entered my life, I ended up walking away from my position as the Assistant Pastor of my church for more than 10 years, and I quit the only church that I loved as my spiritual family. How could this be? This is not what I thought Jesus would do. All of this brought me to an astounding crossroad in my life. Who was this Jesus that was leading me away from my church? Was I really hearing from God? Have I been serving the wrong God in the wrong church all this time? Did I backslide? Or was it all of the above?

Well, you be the judge.

Chapter 1
While Searching for God, Fear Got Me

Motherhood for me began at the age of 19 years old in a country that I never dreamed I would be living in, Germany. When I started out, I was married to a soldier and we both loved each other. But like most newlyweds, we struggled while getting used to one another and suddenly having to raise a family. We had marital problems when my husband and I were just starting out and we ran to the church for help. At first, we both were met with opened arms, love, and such hospitality, and then something happened. After just a few months of joining the church, my husband was shunned by many of the members, and I somehow found myself being one of the main accusers against him. And then through a gradual and shameful process, I found myself in an intimate relationship with the pastor of the church that later turned into adultery.

Honestly, if I had the chance to do it over again, believe me, I would not have done this. It's hard to believe, even today, that I threw my whole marriage away just like that. Adultery was like a type of death that not only happened to our marriage, but something on the inside of me died too.

After much embarrassment and pain, I now understand that being an adulterer is not just a physical sin, but a very serious spiritual sin in the sight of God. In the book of Leviticus, it states that a woman caught in adultery would be killed because the crime was so horrific. "If a man is found sleeping with another man's wife, both the man who slept with her and the woman must die. You must purge the evil from Israel." (Leviticus

20:10, NLT)

According to Harper's Bible Dictionary, *adultery* is defined as voluntary sexual intercourse between one person and another not the lawful spouse, condemned by the law codes and seen as detrimental to family welfare. (1961)

Further, it states that symbolically, adultery expressed the sins of backsliding Israel (Jeremiah 3:8 & Matt 12:39).

Adultery causes separation between us and God. As with all sin, God hates adultery!

I didn't know then, but I definitely know now, that adultery is an evil that not only affects the adulterer, the spouse, and the other outside partner, but it affects your children, the other families involved, and your own soul. It is an abomination in the sight of God, and the magnitude of the consequences is too great to cover in this book.

Marriage according to the Bible is not only sacred, it's also a place or position in which God dwells in order to lead righteous families. It's headed by a husband and wife under the guidance of God. Marriage is not just a ceremony, it's like a command post in a family, and it has incredible power. It would take another book to explain the sacredness of marriage and how God uses it to communicate His will for His people. It's a divine covenant that is strictly for husband, wife, and God Himself. I violated that covenant between my husband and myself, and I also violated the covenant of someone else's marriage. The pastor I committed adultery with was also married.

For many years while in adultery, I lived under the grace of God, not realizing the magnitude of my sin and denial. In retrospect, I believe that my disobedience to God was causing my heart to be more and more deceived and calloused toward everyone I once loved, including God. Adultery is wrong on so many levels, and it has vast consequences, both seen and unseen. God is very serious about marriages that were brought together by Him. What God has joined together, let no man separate

(Matthew 19:6).

At age 19 I knew right from wrong, so there was no excuse for my behavior. What I failed to see was how my wrong was affecting my relationship with God. Pride had gotten such a hold on me that I actually believed that God was okay with my decision to have an affair with the pastor. And for many years, I actually believed that God was the one orchestrating the adulterous encounters. How did I come to believe this? Well, it's interesting.

Believing A Lie…

In order to understand my train of thought concerning the adulterous relationship, I have to first acknowledge how the evil was presented to me in the first place. Just like Eve in the book of Genesis, the devil tempted me with something I longed for, which was attention and relief. It seems that a lot a people, especially those from the older generations. get very uncomfortable when there are real discussions about Satan. I can remember a time when I was a child that I was not allowed to say the words devil or Satan in my relatives' homes. I was told that, "There ain't no devil." It seemed like we were disrespecting the elderly or something by saying the word devil. Nobody ever spoke of the devil in my house.

Even now, when I talk to people who are my peers, we keep the conversations short whenever it comes to talking about the enemy of God (Satan). We'll casually say, "The devil is a lie," or "Satan is busy," but there is no true conversation about the reality of this evil force and what damage it is really doing to people's lives. Oh yeah, we are also very careful to not blame the devil for all of our problems. Some generations are not comfortable with passing the blame on the devil for our own failures and actions. The belief is that we should be accountable for our own mistakes, crimes and failures. To simply say the devil made you do wrong in your life makes you look like you're crazy or just trying to pass the blame. You are not taking responsibility for your own actions.

I agree with some of the ideology above in that not taking ownership or responsibility for our own actions could give us excuses to continue to do them. This type of thinking allows us to hide behind the devil whenever we want to do wrong in our lives. And that's just not right and it's not healthy either. It's just simply wrong.

So, I do not agree that we should try to run from our own actions by simply saying that, "the devil made me do it." However, to say that we came up with evil ideas and actions on our own is not fair to us either. There are many people who have found themselves in horrible situations that they never (in a million years) would have thought they could be in. None of us just woke up one morning and decided to kill, steal, and destroy our own lives along with the lives of others. There was a thought process that caused our actions. Where did the thought come from? Who or what put those thoughts into our heads? I'm just sayin'.

I never intended to do the evil things that I have done in my life. There are people today that have done unimaginable things in their lives, things they never thought they were capable of doing.

Think about this. Some of us give God credit for helping us to accomplish incredible challenges. That's good, right? We know that we had His help. As Christians we are comfortable saying that the good that we do did not come from ourselves. Instead we say that God used us. We also say that the good deeds we do for others come from the God who blessed us. That's true. Knowing this, we realize that we do good based on something greater than ourselves. So, my question is who helped us to accomplish the bad? Who gets the credit for the bad that we do? Did we come up with the bad on our own, or did we have help?

When I look at my grandbaby's little face, and she smiles back at me, it's hard for me to believe that she could be capable of committing homicide or any crime. She may be a little mischievous, but she is no criminal. Well, we all know that as she grows up that sweet little baby will be capable of doing many unthinkable things. God forbid, I hope she never does. All I'm saying is, where did that come from? God does not make criminals, liars, adulterers, haters. You know the rest of the list. These qualities are coming from something other than ourselves. Not all of us want to do bad, hateful things, but sometimes we do. Paul states it best in Romans chapter 7.

If good comes from something greater, why can't we see that bad comes from something greater than ourselves too? That is, it comes from Satan. Now listen. I know that the devil did not make me pack up and leave my husband. I did that on my own, but I'm telling you that something evil was present with me when I did leave. People who knew me back then could tell that something was different about me and it was not good. My whole attitude and even my appearance changed years before I left my family and followed this church from Germany. Well, maybe you can be the judge as I reveal other strange things to you in the next chapters. But first let me apologize before I give you the details of my experience. I realize that for some of you, talking about Satan is offensive and others feel that by doing so, I'm giving glory to him. Some of you continue to deny that he is even real even in the face of evidence. How wrong you are if you think that we should keep silent about something that is very present and very real.

Please allow me to veer off again for a moment. I want to illustrate my point further. My husband was a scout in the United States Army, serving as a sergeant in one of the toughest jobs in the military. I'm ashamed to say that it took me a long time to realize just how much danger my husband was in as he was being trained and later fought in the Dessert Storm War.

A scout's mission was to go into enemy territory first before the rest of the Army got there. As scouts, they would get as close to the enemy's camp as possible without being detected while carrying tons and tons of artillery (explosives, tanks, machine guns, etc.) Their assignment was to report directly to the General any valuable information they learned about the enemy. This included the location, number of armed men, women and children, the types of weapons, the enemy's movements, habits, and any other details about the actual land. Scouts were the front-line soldiers which meant they would be killed first (before the rest of the team), especially if they walked into a trap unknowingly. I guess you could say they were the first to spy and the first to die. It was their job and they took it seriously. (A little note to my husband: thank you, for your service to our country, babe!)

Any information about the enemy was necessary in order to build strategies, keep control, and protect the US from enemy invasion. Needless to say, the information they provided to the General was ABSOLUTELY critical. They were trying to win a war! The military fought and won wars based on the information about the enemy given to them by the scouts.

Why is it that Christians, who are soldiers for Christ, refuse information about their enemy? The information is not designed to bring glory to their enemy. It is designed to strengthen God's team and help protect us from traps and attacks (2Corinthians 2:11b).

It doesn't make sense to refuse valuable information that is edifying to the church. Does it?

Well, maybe that's it.

Some Christians do not think they are in a war even though the Bible clearly says that we are, and our weapons are not physical but spiritual. (2 Cor 10:4, KJV) Many people are *called* Christians, but not all of us *are* Christian. Many of us *go* to church, but not all of us *are* the church.
The true worshippers of God need information to win the battles that are in our lives. We know that the end result is that God has won the war against Satan; however, the everyday battles that God leaves for us to win in our personal lives are being lost. Why? Because some of us refuse to learn, discuss and put on the whole armor of God. And how do you put on the whole armor, by FIRST having the right information.

Because of the lack of knowledge (and wisdom to correctly apply the knowledge), our families are suffering needlessly, and many of God's people are getting spiritually slaughtered by the forces of darkness daily.

Drugs, violence, sexual perversion, pride, evil lusts, the pleasure we take in hating one another, the love of money are not just killing the ungodly; they are wiping out the Christians too! We cannot afford to keep blaming our leaders anymore. Although many are to blame, we cannot simply continue to bash our teachers or parents. If our leaders are not teaching us, **then we have to teach ourselves the truth**. We must read and study the Bible to find out what it says for ourselves. WE ARE IN A WAR!!! Again, it is not my intent to offend you or give glory to the enemy, but I believe the Bible which teaches the fact that we are dealing with an enemy that will not stop until all of us are in bondage to him. I don't know about you, but I am convinced that we are in a spiritual war.

To not be able to talk about an enemy that personally tried to kill me and the people I love equals bondage. And, sorry my friends, I will not be placed in that type of bondage, so please forgive me as I speak about this enemy.

His name is Satan, and he has many faces. He is behind all of the evil we see today. He was behind the adultery that I committed and the lifestyle that followed.

In order for the people of God to avoid being tricked by the devil's schemes and falling into his traps, it is necessary to identify Satan constantly, quickly and accurately. I fell into his trap when I was only 19 years old. Everything decent, everything sensible, everything wholesome and everything pure in my life went right out the window because Satan presented to me a "perfect" situation, and I accepted the deal.

Here's the twist. I was raised with a loving mom who made sure that I went to good schools and had a well-rounded academic education. As a teenager, I was even on the honor roll almost every year, attending college prep courses at the University of Chicago campus while assisting my mom in her own business as her office clerk (at age 15). There was no doubt I was on my way to becoming a doctor because I had strong examples of successful people around me, namely my mom.

I had lofty dreams. Most of my family was made up of entrepreneurs, teachers, and artists. Almost all of us either had college degrees or were working towards them. Also, I was introduced to many powerful, dynamic community leaders who were awesome movers and shakers. They too believed in my dream to become a doctor. I was constantly surrounded by successful black people. And, without a doubt, I was headed for medical school and had already finished my first year of college by the time I fell into the trap of the devil.

My passion to be a doctor mainly stemmed from the duty to proudly represent my African American heritage, so I was geared up, locked and loaded. The first step was to just get through four years of college, and I was up for the task, except for one thing.

Still, in all of that, I was a prime candidate for Satan. I had something in me that a college education could not get rid of. It was called selfish ambition.

I didn't know it then, but the type of ambition I had was sinful. I was willing to do whatever it took to be the best and keep up a good image.

Although I didn't attend church every Sunday, I'm grateful that my mother and grandmother encouraged me to have a relationship with God when I was younger. That was the only thing that helped me when I got older and was finally tired of my sin. In Proverbs 22:6 it says to train up a child in the way he should go and when he is old, he will not depart from it. That was true for me because after the horrible ordeal in my life, I did not walk back, but I ran back to God!

Before getting married, I left home as a young adult wanting to know and love God, but when Satan presented the "perfect situation" to me, everything I learned just seemed to vanish. I couldn't remember what I was taught, I couldn't remember what I wanted to do with my life, I couldn't remember my dreams, I couldn't remember anything!

Becoming a doctor was not the problem. The problem was that I was willing to give up my true identity for a false one. In order to be accepted into this new relationship at this church, my ambition shifted. I no longer wanted the life I had with my husband and children. I wanted the recognition, attention and security that I could gain by being a part of this religious family. It seemed good, it seemed godly, so I accepted the offer to become one of them.

Suddenly, I was hooked because Satan concocted other temptations that I was dreaming about inside. Somehow, it seemed that he knew my private thoughts. No one ever told me about Satan when I was a child; all I knew about was God. I never knew that there was a force that hated God and mankind so much that he would transform himself into an angel of light in order to deceive me. When I did hear about Satan being the enemy of God, I figured that I didn't do anything to Satan, so why should I have to worry about him? The problem was not between Satan and me. It was between God and Satan. I figured that I wasn't a problem to the devil, so why would he need to trick or bother me? That was my line of thinking back then.

To be honest, if anyone would have told me back then that Satan existed, I would have veered away from them. "You're crazy. Don't get me caught up in that, I'm too intelligent to believe in invisible ghosts," would have been my response. Back then, Satan was just a cartoon figure on TV and nobody in my house ever mentioned him. When I was a teenager, I even went to a numerologist named Venus. It was just for fun. I remember that she was going to read my palm one day. I didn't take it seriously; I was just excited to let her to do a reading. I remember that on that day she started the reading, she just stopped abruptly and left. Everything was quiet.

It was a little weird, but I just shrugged it off. What happened? I don't know. Whatever happened at that session was unclear. I was a kid; I didn't know any better.

After having experienced what I have as an adult, I now realize why it wasn't such a good idea to get that reading. Now I know that just having that one encounter with her, who used familiar spirits and witchcraft, opened a door in my life to the occult. The Bible warns us to stay away from evil like this, but like I said, I didn't know. Although I never practiced in the occult, the mere experience with palm reading invited unwelcome spiritual influences into my life.

Today I see that this encounter opened a door that allowed the enemy to terrorize my life for the next several years. I 'm sure that's why the Bible warns us to eschew (deliberately avoid) evil, even the very appearance of it.

And let me tell you, I was not prepared. I wonder how many are like I was. Are you? I wonder if there are those reading this book thinking that Satan is a joke. If so, you better think again.

Believe it or not, it was a trap that cost me 28 years of my life. And those years I will never get back again.

So, yeah, I'm going to talk about Satan because somebody is falling into his trap somewhere today, and with the help of the Lord, I want to prevent that.

After accepting the "perfect situation," I engaged in a battle with Satan for my soul. Gradually, I was being tormented and molded under witchcraft and was unaware. Being slowly molded into a minister of Satan, I nearly lost my mind, until one day I stopped and called God for help. I called on the God that my mom and grandmother had talked about when I was a child. Believe me when I say that what we, as parents, instill in our children may one day save their lives. This time when I prayed, I also listened to God with all ears, and I finally obeyed what the Lord was telling me to do even though it was not popular.

I have learned that as children of God we must pray, but we also need to obey what God says to us. Pray and obey!

The following chapters lay out the perfect plan that Satan tried to use to win my soul.

Chapter 2
Doubt and The Great Divide

There was something very charming and powerful about Pastor Menard that first got my attention. He said the right stuff; he carried himself with swag and confidence. He was young and good looking and spoke with authority. I dreamed about this kind of man ever since I was a teenager. He seemed intelligent and acted as if he knew me even though I had never met him before, but instantly he seemed to understand my needs and my desires. The desires I had, he wanted them too. I couldn't believe that some of the experiences we had as kids were the same, and it seemed like he could read my mind. He knew how to address things in me that were private (things only God knew in my prayers). I was curious about how he understood me so well.

The views I had about life, he had them too. He wanted what I wanted, and he always stood for truth. I liked the fact that the truth was always what he demanded from everybody as the pastor, and he made it easy for me be myself. I felt comfortable telling him the truth about everything in my life. I didn't mind telling him my true feelings about things that happened to me in the past.

All of these qualities are what first got my attention about him. But the one thing that really got my attention was the fact that he was the kind of man that believed in the rights of women. I came from a family of strong women with strong opinions about women as leaders. Up to this point in my life, I had never met a man who seemed to support women having their own minds and being self-sufficient. This blew my mind.

In his church, I was also intrigued by the type of men who were around him. There were just a few brothers of the church, but they acted like they really respected him. They seemed like they would lay down their lives for the pastor. Pastor Menard seemed to be training them as young brothers, and they were his loyal protectors and main supporters. On the other hand, the women in the church (some of whom were the wives of the brothers) were different. They appeared quiet and always willing to serve the church. They seemed devoted.

After getting to know him, Pastor Menard told me that the women wanted to be close to him. He came across as if he was annoyed by the fact that the women seemed to want to be his main supporters too. He seemed to only want the brothers to have that role; he was only pacifying the women by being nice to them. He didn't have time be emotional. He was like a commander ready to lead a no-nonsense church, and women were too soft and needed too much attention, but he still supported women as leaders. A year after I was there, he appointed a female to one of his assistant pastor positions and another female as one of the associate ministers. Although he was nicer to all the females, and much firmer with the brothers of the church, he seemed to have a genuine interest in surrounding himself with strong leaders.

He often talked about how he was trying to teach men how to be leaders in their own homes. In general, the women were to be supporters to their husbands as the husbands were supporters to the church. There were approximately five or 10 families already members of this church by the time I and my husband arrived.

One of the most incredible things about Pastor Menard was the fact he could and would solve problems without hesitation. Families would go to him for family counseling, advice, marital concerns, help with food, and even money. He was like a father and provider for his church members. Members seemed to love and respect him.

After seeing how others were unashamed to go to the pastor, I and my husband learned to trust Pastor Menard too. He was like a mentor to my husband, and Mrs. Menard was like a mentor to me. We were learning to fit in with our new Christian family.

As I can recollect, there was never a time that I felt he would not be able to help us. So, like the other families, my husband and I received counseling, guidance, support, and sometimes food or money if necessary. Although he did not always have money right away, Pastor Menard had access to it, and he had some way that we could earn it. For example, I used to provide babysitting for his two daughters while his wife went to work. I got paid and learned a lot about housekeeping from his wife.

Having this church family while living in a foreign land, I felt I had what I needed with no strings attached. He seemed to enjoy being the spiritual leader for us and the rest of the members without much in return.

As I began to have individual counseling with Pastor Menard, one of the things that made me especially fond of him was the fact that he was concerned about my personal goals.

He encouraged me to pursue what I wanted in life and he was there to support me. His advice sounded like that of a dad to his daughter, and he built me up as if I mattered to him. He even had other people help me, though sometimes I felt like a burden. For example, a few of the members would look out for me when my husband was away on a military assignment. They would invite us over for dinner when we didn't have much to eat.

Pastor Menard had a way of bringing the fun into the room. I knew when he came around that there would be good food, excitement. and a sense of "Everything was gonna be okay." He was the life of the Christian fellowship dinners.

All in all, he knew exactly the words to say that gave me hope. By his gentle words and his gentle tone when he spoke to me, I could not help but imagine that he was how a father and husband were supposed to be.

He listened attentively, not just to my words, but also to my feelings. He understood both, and I felt comfortable telling him stuff I would never share with anyone else but my husband or best friend. He made me feel that what he was to me, was what I was to him.

He used to publicly acknowledge how loyal my husband and I were to his church. One day in a one-on-one session, he called me his dream girl and said no other women had what I had; I was rare and special. He said that he was grateful to God that God would allow him to have me in his life as his friend and a member of his church.

Those were his actual words, and I played those words over and over in my mind thinking that God had answered my prayers too. I loved the attention.

During this time, my husband and I had only been married for almost a year, and although we were having some marital problems, I loved my husband. Before I met Pastor Menard, I believed that my husband was the man that God had for me and I was happy with that. However, when I heard the words of Pastor Menard, he spoke the things right out of my dreams. I saw his charm and the qualities he had, and I began to be curious. Before long, I began to question the marriage I had with my husband. Somehow, I had become confused and I began to compare what my husband was doing and saying to what Pastor Menard was doing and saying. It looked like my husband was missing something. My husband started looking different to me. Everything started looking different. And I concluded that maybe God didn't give me my husband after all. I began to think that maybe it was a mistake that I was married to my husband. I couldn't shake the thoughts.

After that doubt about my husband, I began questioning everything and everyone in my life. I felt like I was wrong for the life I had with my husband, and even the relationship I had with my own biological family didn't seem that necessary to me anymore. After this realization, I guess it was easy to desire Pastor Menard instead of my husband. I even began to have mixed feelings about my upbringing and all the friends I used to know. Also, my personal goals changed directions and seemed to be only for this church. I found myself wanting what the church wanted. I wanted to excel in this church, and that became my obsession. My desires were slowly shifting in a new direction. I firmly believed that Pastor Menard was a man of God and I wanted to show my support and loyalty to him and the church members. Unexpectedly, I even started desiring Pastor Menard and even believed that God was telling me that the pastor was my true husband.

And it didn't matter that Pastor Menard was already married because I was willing to wait for my turn. It seemed like he knew how to be what I longed for in a friend, father, brother, leader and husband. Pastor Menard had my complete attention, and I became whatever he wanted me to be. In my mind, I knew this had to be God who was blessing me in my life, and at that time nobody could tell me any different.

Unfortunately, it took me some time and a lot of tears to recognize that from the moment I allowed Pastor Menard into my life, I was under the control of witchcraft! The reason that I now understand that it was witchcraft was because the most noted presence I felt from that point on was fear coupled with anxiety, confusion and forgetfulness. There was an overwhelming sense of fear in my house, in my thoughts, my sleep and especially in my marriage. It was a fear that no matter what I did, I could not explain it nor shake it.

Witchcraft is "the practice of magic, especially black magic; the use of spells and the invocation of spirits." (Harper's Bible Dictionary)

"Witchcraft works fluently through dirty hearts." (The Demon Dictionary, Kimberly Daniels)

Witchcraft spirits are "spirits of rebellion that cause a person to operate in a power outside of the realm of the true and living God." (The Demon Dictionary, Kimberly Daniels)

"A witch's power is obtained through contact with evil spirits." (Harper's

Bible Dictionary)

"The power or practice of witches, sorcery, black magic; bewitching attraction or charm, enchantment, irresistible influence, fascination" (Webster New Universal Unabridged, 1979)

"A drug (spell-giving potion), a druggist-pharmacist, poisoner, magician, sorcerer" (Strong's concordance # 5332)

After only having been in the church for approximately three months, I was already experiencing profound isolation from my biological family and a great division between me and my husband. My husband became a stranger to me and I didn't know why.

Chapter 3
"Lies and Promises Were Lookin' Good"

When we first joined the church, I remember that Pastor Menard was trying to help me and my husband through some rough times in our marriage. The pastor made me believe that he was going to not only train my husband to be like the other brothers in the church, but also train my husband to be a strong leader like himself. Then the talks and training began. My husband was listening and was trying to become a deacon in the church. The brotherhood in the church appeared to be strong. It seemed that all the brothers were trying to pass tests and complete some type of training to become leaders.

After some time there, Pastor Menard told me that God was allowing me to serve him in a special relationship.

I kept thinking to myself, I thought God was going to help my husband, but from this I could see that God wanted me to serve pastor Menard instead. He said that his wife didn't understand his needs like I did. He said I was the only one in his life that had all the good qualities of his wife and all the professional qualities of his secretary wrapped into one. He said that I had to have a certain type of faith to be in a relationship with him like this. He also said that I was the only one he ever allowed to get close to him and serve his needs except for his secretary. He said that he and his secretary were very good friends and that I would never take her place, but I was the next closest person to him after his wife. He said he would never leave or hurt his wife, but that if he were not married, I would be his choice. He said that I was his dream girl, the girl he always wanted. All of this made me feel like I was number one. It was a feeling of acceptance that I never knew before.

Basking in all of this attention, I was willing to believe anything from Pastor Menard, and then the bomb hit. I received some news that made my heart sink to a low that I'd never felt. Pastor Menard said that my husband only married me for sex and not love. He said that my husband thought that I was a burden and was only staying with me because he had to. He told me that my husband was eventually going to leave me when we got back to the United States and that I was going to be raising my kids alone unless I did something about it.

The pastor said that my husband didn't care about me like he (the pastor) did. He said that my husband didn't know my worth like he did. Repeatedly he told me that my husband didn't want me. Pastor Menard said he knew these things because of what my husband had confessed to him privately.

He told me that my husband was having sex with other women. I was frozen in fear when he told me this. Pastor Menard said that he was there to protect me from my husband, and I couldn't confront my husband because it was a private confession just between the two of them. Because I could not address these things with my husband, I kept them inside for years. Each time I looked at my husband, I wondered what woman he was with. More and more, I hated to be around him as suspicions of him being with someone else were eating me up inside. As time went on, I grew more and more resentful towards him and it showed.

Pastor Menard offered me an alternative. He said that I could be in a relationship with him that God allowed. However, in order to do so, I would have to stop having sex with my husband altogether and devote myself to him (the pastor) and God's business. He made me believe that having sex with my husband somehow made me dirty and undesirable. He also convinced me that having sex with my husband was a sin since my husband was not saved like the rest of us. Although he was trying to become one of the deacons, my husband was not submitting to the ways of the church yet. He was offering me a chance to become more a part of his team through this special relationship.

Furthermore, Pastor Menard said I would have to earn my way into being his best friend (just like his secretary did) by doing better for him than his secretary. I had to work harder than she did to be a close friend. Close friends got privileges.

After several months of talking and sharing with me, he cautioned me that this close relationship was only for a few people and I should not to try to act like I was his wife. Otherwise, he would embarrass me in public. He made it clear that he loved his wife although he was fond of me too. He was not willing to hurt her because God wouldn't like it. He told me that if I ever let others know of this secret relationship and ended up hurting his wife, then God would not allow us to work together. I was to understand that our relationship was approved by God, but it was private.

Also, with what appeared to be a streak of jealousy, he said, jokingly, that if he just thought that I was laughing and having a good time with my husband, he would hurt me. I didn't take this seriously; I didn't believe he would really hurt me. But I did notice that he was very jealous at times. He regularly said (in a joking way) that he would hurt me if I tried to leave him. He also said that if at any time I wanted to get out of this relationship, then all I needed to do was to tell him that God told me to leave. I continued with this arrangement and I never heard God say to leave. As a matter of fact, I never heard anything from God outside of Pastor Menard. All of my thoughts pertaining to God had to go through Pastor Menard. He encouraged me to tell everything to him. I regularly shared anything I felt God was saying to me with Pastor Menard, and he always interpreted God's messages for me. That's the way it was for a very long time. As I learned the norms of this relationship, I gained favor with the members and seemed to be finding my place in his ministry.

Things seemed to be going well for a while. I was excited to be appointed as Assistant Secretary of the church and in charge of small tasks. As a result, we began to work closely with each other. One of my duties was to help organize the membership registration process for our church and sister churches while privately I became one of his best friends. He confided in me.

Being his friend meant that I received help with my personal needs quicker than the rest of the members. I didn't have a lot of clothes, so I would receive used clothes from the church or pastor's wife. Not everyone was allowed to care for the pastor's kids. I got chosen to babysit his children to make a little extra money that would help get things that my husband's money could not buy. I was taken care of, and Pastor Menard would remind me that he was the one making this happen for me. He said the congregation trusted him and members did what he said. He was the one telling them to help me.

Everything stayed like this until one day I made a huge decision to disobey Pastor Menard by having intercourse with my husband. He found out because he questioned my husband one day.

Soon, Pastor Menard began treating me as if I had been disloyal to him. He emotionally ignored me for days, and I was in turmoil because I felt that I sinned against him and God. Emotionally and mentally tormented by what I had done, I couldn't live with the guilt and shame in knowing that I had disappointed him. I also felt that God was angry with me too. To get relief, I decided to confess and prove my devotion and loyalty to him even more. Sometimes I didn't want to, though. There were so many unanswered questions like: why was God mad at me for having intercourse with my own husband? After all, I was still married to him. I wanted to be intimate with my husband, but was my husband really cheating like Pastor Menard said? I still desired my husband; was it ok to desire my husband even though he was not saved? When will my husband and I ever love each other again? What will Pastor Menard do if he ever knew that I still loved my husband? Is this wrong what I am doing with Pastor Menard? Why do I feel so confused all the time? Although tormented, I chose to throw myself into the church. I kept busy. This kept my mind on something else for a while.

Slowly, I started withdrawing from my husband and becoming more determined to work for the church, even when it sometimes caused conflict. Working for the church made me feel less dirty. When I was busy at church, I had some relief from all of the questions in my head.

From this point on, I had become a different person, always depressed, quiet, hateful and defensive toward my husband. Although enduring what felt like oppression and stress, I ended up conceiving my second pregnancy with my husband. To my surprise, I was pregnant with twins while still caring for my daughter who was still in diapers. My emotions were all over the place. I guessed that most of my emotions were attributed to me being pregnant, so I figured they would pass once my twins were born. To top it off, my husband also became withdrawn from me, and for some reason, he did not associate with the church like he used to except on some occasions.

However, I continued to go, even though there was always friction at home. We could not talk calmly to one another mainly because I constantly felt that if he was not saved, then I could not associate with him. Besides that, I was always afraid the pastor would find out if I was nice to him. You see, sometimes the pastor seemed to be checking on me by asking my husband how things were at home. I guess the pastor wanted to see how I was acting toward my husband when he was not around. I don't know.

Anxiously, I thought that if I was being loving with my husband at home, that meant I was compromising with a sinner. Therefore, I had to be "holy" around my husband in order to draw him to salvation. Well, that's what I was taught in the church. Back then, holy to me meant to be separated from and unfriendly to those who were not saved. We were not supposed to mingle with the unsaved.

In all of this, Pastor Menard told me that what we had in this secret relationship was not sin. He said that by faith, I would need to find my own peace with this arrangement. And I found a little peace with it. I believed that God was answering my prayers by allowing me to be one of the pastor's closest friends.

As a minister, the pastor seemed to still be concerned about my husband's soul, and he even at times acted like he was interested in saving my marriage and drawing my husband to salvation. It was back and forth like this - very confusing. I still wanted to be with my husband even though I kept thinking that something was drawing me away from my husband at the same time. Pastor Menard seemed to support my marriage on one hand and then get angry with me for showing feelings for my husband on the other hand. This whole arrangement was a little weird to me, but I was new to the ways of the church and the teachings. All I knew was that I wanted to be accepted, I wanted to fit in. The pastor and the church were my emotional support.

My husband didn't know the real reason for the pastor's questions. Neither did I at first. What was true was that if I was nice to my husband, the pastor would shun me, telling me that I was being gullible. Consequently, I constantly lived in fear that I was being a "stupid woman" anytime I showed affection towards my husband and family. According to Pastor Menard, a "stupid woman" was a woman who compromised with the devil, especially in her husband. And we were never to compromise with the enemy.

I hated being called stupid, so I constantly fought to keep myself emotionally distant from anyone who was not one of us (a member of our church).

Pastor Menard had a way of openly rebuking me or anyone who disagreed with his suggestions or warnings from the Lord. If our feelings from God did not match with his feelings, then we were openly rebuked (corrected) in front of the congregation. And for weeks we would be shunned by other members who agreed with the pastor. Any who opposed were made to feel guilty, humiliated and like outsiders until the pastor accepted you back into his favor. He said he did this on behalf of God. Pastor Menard had such command and authority whenever he rebuked anyone. It almost seemed theatrical. After I was openly rebuked one time for not agreeing with the pastor, I tried not to ever do it again. I couldn't bear the long weeks of what seemed to be emotional torture having to hear how I disrespected him. As a matter of fact, he and others continued to remind me of my disrespect to the pastor even years later. The way I was shunned was by being ignored when I came into a room or seeing that some members refused to engage in conversations with me. There was tension and the atmosphere was filled with disapproval as if I were a criminal or traitor against the church and pastor. It was horrible and hard to ignore. It seemed I would never live it down, but eventually I did.

Knowing how humiliating it was for me to live under constant disdain by the members, I could only imagine how my husband must have felt when it happened to him. The church members began to shun my husband whenever I confessed my frustration about my husband to the pastor. After confession, the pastor would make open statements that "somebody in the church" was having marital problems. He would talk about how that family was out of the will of God for "one of the spouses" not confessing their sins. It was so much pressure that if you were guilty, you would squirm in your seat. It wasn't hard to figure out that it was my husband and me that the pastor was talking about because the church membership at this time was fairly small, and during my pregnancy I especially looked sad and troubled when I came to church. My husband was shunned many times.

After I learned to be more compliant and accepting of the church norms, I was back into Pastor Menard's favor. Being in his favor meant that all of the members were especially accepting of me too. The ones who shunned my husband were always looking for Pastor Menard's approval to either accept my husband back or continue to reject him. It was weird, but I became accustomed to it. However, there were some members who would just step back and say nothing. They stared in silence.

I felt justified in joining in with the shunning against my husband because I was also plagued with the idea that he was always lying to me. I never trusted him, even in the smallest matters. We were strangers in our own home. I made sure that I would not say or do anything that would make the Pastor, or my husband think that I had any feelings for him. I had turned cold inside (all in the name of God). I kept hearing the words in my head that said that my husband did not want me, he was a liar, he was unsaved. These thoughts followed me day and night. Even when there were times where I wanted to give in and talk to him, I quickly reverted back to the recurring thoughts in my head. Sometimes I was almost in a panic whenever he and I were alone. I was fighting to hide my feelings of love and my need to be intimate with him. Deep inside, I wanted to love him and be close, but each time I thought to, I began to think it was a sin to even have those thoughts of wanting my husband. Instead, I just continued to ignore him as I listened to the thoughts that kept me angry with him all the time.

Even when I didn't do anything purposely to offend the pastor, I always felt that I was doing something wrong anyway. Pastor Menard always watched me in public when I was with my husband. I couldn't help but notice how the pastor's eyes looked odd when he stared at me, but somehow, I just kept dismissing it. I'll never forget his long stares at me, with eyes that looked dark and cold.

For the next three years, it seemed that many unusual things kept happening. There was often no explanation for them. Here are a few odd things I remember.

- There seemed to be a presence in my house that felt evil. I could sense it in the living room at various times, but I didn't know what it was nor what to do.

- When the twins were born, various strangers (from random places) would come up to me and say, "There's something about those boys. They are here for a reason." No one could ever explain that.

- My mother-in-law and her sister visited us in Germany after the babies were born. I remember being really troubled with them being there. I felt that I was doing something wrong by having them in my house since they were sinners. While they were visiting, the pastor would make comments about how it was against God to associate with family members and miss church services. I was so stressed. The church members would shun me when I missed church and I missed a day when my in-laws came to visit. I was falling apart because I kept feeling that I was in trouble for having them in my home, so I remember I began to speak in tongues trying to pray them away. Unknowingly, I created an atmosphere that was unbearable for them and within a few days they packed up and left back to the States. I was so relieved because the punishment in my head stopped when they left, but my heart yearned for them to help me make sense of what was happening to me. Nonetheless, my attitude was so strange and rude, and I don't know why I was so mean towards them. I kept reflecting on the fact that I and my mother-in-law used to have a good relationship before I left Chicago. However, since being in Germany, I regarded her as my enemy, and I could not explain it. When my in-laws returned to the States, they told others that they were very concerned about what was happening. They viewed me as a fanatic. Thinking that they and others were discussing me made me even more angry. I disconnected from them all together.

- Freak accidents would happen out of nowhere that either caused injuries or almost took the lives of my sons, but each time we always recovered.

I had spent nearly three years in West Germany, partly while the church was there and the last year without the church. Eventually, the church and pastor left Germany and relocated to the States.

Before he left for the States, Pastor Menard came by when I was alone at home one day. I had the strangest conversation with him.

During this time, I had missed several weeks of church (after I gave birth to my sons) and I was really in bad shape emotionally. Without much hesitation, Pastor Menard told me that I would spiritually die without his ministry. He said that it was vital that I moved to the church's new location in the United States.

He further told me that he was especially concerned about my sons, who would definitely die without his ministry too. He said something terrible was going to happen to them. He said the boys had a special call from God and the devil wanted them dead. He said that if they grew up under the wrong hands, they would be extreme criminals, but that with the right leadership they would be used by God. Pastor Menard said he was the only one who could help them, and he hoped that me and my husband would rejoin his church for the sake of my family. Furthermore, he told me that my husband was going to eventually abandon me and he (the pastor) was the only hope for saving him, me, and my kids. All I could do was cry. I was filled with such fear that no words could express what this had done to me.

With three babies all in diapers, I already struggled each day to keep myself looking decent, and depression was an on-going battle I faced. But nothing topped off what happened all in about 10 minutes of my life. In my mind, I felt like my family just received a death sentence, and my whole world seemed to start collapsing.

He also began to interpret a dream I shared with him. It was a dream about me turning into a beast/monster. The dream totally spooked me, and I didn't understand what the warning was. In his interpretation, Pastor Menard said that as long I was out of his church, I would be unsaved and eventually would turn into that beast I saw in my dream. Oh my God! The fear that overwhelmed me left me feeling completely numb! What's happening? What's really going on?

I can't express to you how devastating this moment was for me. He not only told me these things, but he yelled them at me. I guess I showed no emotion while he was talking because the next thing I knew, he was screaming all of this to the top of his lungs. Shocked at his forcefulness, I figured that he was really trying to get me to listen. Well it worked.

After that, he just left the house without saying another word.

All I remember was breaking down while sitting on my couch, and then standing in front of the mirror feeling so numb that literally I couldn't feel myself pinching my skin. I couldn't feel anything.

That was another turning point for me. I thought to myself that I had to stay in his church otherwise I was not going be saved. From that day on, I concluded that I was running for my life. I wanted to tell my husband, but I thought he would not understand. He wasn't into the church like I was, and he stopped talking to the pastor like he did in the beginning. My husband started missing a lot of church, and it was not only because he was working away from home a lot. He seemed to always have reasons to stop participating in the church. He just stayed away from it, sometimes for months.

The other church members (although not fully trusting them all) were now my family because I believed that my biological family had abandoned me. But even the church members would not understand what I was going through. Besides, it was horrifying to the tell church folks that something was falling apart inside of me. I didn't want to look like I was backsliding. I kept going back and forth on what I felt. But finally, I came to grips with the idea that the pastor was right. He really was the only friend I had.

This war in trying to come to grips with believing the words of Pastor Menard became my private hell, but each day I was more and more convinced that I had to remain in Pastor Menard's church in order to be saved. Before long, nothing was going to stop me. And nothing did. Consistently, I was a nervous wreck in getting to church even when there were times I should have just stayed home. There were times I was physically exhausted, and sometimes the kids were sick, or my husband just needed me home. No! I was not going to stay at home. I dragged myself and sick kids to church. If my husband did not go with me, I was unfriendly to him (thinking I was doing the will of God). Over time, I didn't miss a day of church, and I became more and more busy for the church until the pastor and his family left for the States. I worked as the assistant secretary, head of the choir and as a member of the woman's group. I believed I was doing the right thing for the family by being busy in the church. I was saving them.

When Pastor Menard and his family left, the church, as I knew it, was no longer there. Some of the members also moved somewhere else and there was a new pastor assigned. My husband and I remained there with a few other church members.

My husband and I were still having arguments that led us to separate for a few months.

We became strangers and roommates living in what seemed to be a loveless relationship. Daily, I cried about everything. I was mad about everything and most of all, I was constantly living in fear of having a mental breakdown. My dependency on the church had become a way of life. I survived on every word the pastor told me. But when the time came that he and his family had to relocate to the States because his military assignment was finished in Germany, I was becoming increasingly anxious and eventually spiraled into a depression. He invited all the families to join him in the United States to reorganize the church there. A few families pledged to move to the new location. My husband was undecided.

The pastor and his family left, but my husband and I could not leave yet. The military did not release my husband at that time. While still living in Germany, there was an urge in me so strong to get back with the church that it seemed that I felt death on my heels if I didn't. It was an obsession I never knew before.

Feeling abandoned, drifting from one day to the next without a purpose, I felt condemned all the time. It was as if I was sinning by being stuck in a loveless relationship with my husband.

I was not happy with the new pastor assigned to the church. Honestly, it wasn't anything that he did wrong. I just didn't feel comfortable getting used to another pastor. However, trying to feel normal again, I tried attending the church with the new pastor. Unfortunately, there was no hope; I couldn't wait to leave Germany and move to California to rejoin my church in its new location.

Overall, so much had happened where I didn't trust my husband at all, and all I wanted to do was leave Germany at any cost. Every attempt to leave, however, was blocked by the fact that I had to have my husband's approval before the Army would release me to go back to the States. My husband and I fought off and on about whether we would rejoin our old church when his military assignment ended in a few months. I begged him to get reassigned in the state where the church was, and he kept changing his mind. Enraged, mentally exhausted, and utterly desperate, I became more and more hateful towards him. I remember being so depressed that nothing in life was enjoyable at all.

There were so many mixed emotions within me, but all of them amounted to the fact that I didn't want that message to be true that Pastor Menard told me. If I didn't get back with the church, I just knew that I would spiritually die. And there was still a part of me that wanted the special relationship I had with the pastor. He made me feel that I was loved and accepted.

Also tugging at me, there was a part of me that wanted to be happily married to my husband, and then there was a part of me that wanted to give up and die. But what I wanted more was for the thoughts of suicide and the darkness in my mind to just go away. I was tormented every day and could not explain it. How could everyone I ever loved now be strangers to me? My mom, sisters, friends, husband, they were all slowly being erased from my heart. I felt a loneliness and a void that I could not relieve.

Going to the Army chaplain one day, I explained how I felt trapped and needed help. He said that I should check into a mental institute. That's what I wanted to avoid! Why is this Chaplain telling me this? Am I going crazy? Everywhere I turned, there was someone blaming me for my own condition.

I realized quickly that while the church was my support system, the military personnel was my husband's support, not mine. The Army personnel all agreed with him, and many times, any paperwork I needed to leave Germany was either delayed or denied. It seemed that roadblocks were everywhere. Why were my husband and these people trying to keep me here? I couldn't understand it.

It was an affliction I never knew. I prayed as much as I could but even my relationship with God depended on the pastor. I kept thinking that without the pastor's teaching, how could I reach God?

I finally concluded that my husband was ultimately trying to keep me from the church so that I would die a sinner. With this in mind, I devised ways to escape. While still in Germany, I even moved in with some church friends who were still there with us, just to get away from my husband. That lasted for about a month.

It wasn't until I agreed to go home to Chicago to visit my mom that he signed the papers for my (and my children's) airplane flight back to the United States. I was supposed to stay at my mom's house and wait for him to join me. Later, he was going to join the kids and me in Chicago, but I flipped the script.

Feeling like I was running for my life, I felt that I literally escaped from Germany and ended up in Chicago visiting my mom. My mom didn't know that secretly I was headed for California without my husband. I was filled with so much anxiety and fear that I felt that the only way to be "normal" was to be with my church which had relocated to California. It was as if I was looking for a religious fix and if I didn't have it, I would mentally and spiritually fall apart.

While back in Chicago

When the kids and I arrived at my mom's house, it was not hard to see that I was a different person. By this time, I had been gone from her house about two and a half years. My family knew there was something strange about me, and I knew it too. For me things felt different at my mom's house. However, we all tried to act as cordial as possible. My mom appeared happy to see me and the kids. I couldn't find any fault in her except that I was repeatedly taunted in my mind with the thoughts that she was a sinner and that the pastor told me not to trust anyone who was not saved like us. So, I misled my mom and didn't tell her that I had other thoughts to leave before my husband came to join us at her house. He was going to join us in Chicago in about two months.

Frantically, while staying with my mom for a few weeks, I planned my trip to leave Chicago for California where I believed I would be 'saved.' Nothing was going to stop me, not even the love of my mother. I didn't even stop to visit my mother-in-law who was also in Chicago. Now I regret it, but I had already written her off as an enemy back then. To be honest, I don't remember anything she did wrong except she too was a sinner and I had to stay away from her. Embarrassed at the idea of being labeled as a fanatic, I treated her with resentment. Nonetheless, my mother-in-law was not aware that I was in Chicago and leaving for California. Little did any of us know that she would never see me or her grandchildren until 15 years later.

Meanwhile, I was staying at my mother's house for a few weeks. A few days prior to departing to California, I told my mom that I would be leaving. She seemed to be in disbelief and tried to reason with me to change my mind. She really could not see how I was going to make a three-day trip alone with three babies on the road. I don't think she fully understood how much I had changed and what I was willing to do. I didn't explain many of the situations that happened in Germany except for the fact that the pastor was great. Literally, almost every word that came from my mouth centered on how good the pastor was to my family. My mom pleaded and begged me to stay and tried to help me see how my decision was very irrational, but I didn't listen.

On the day of my departure at 5 a.m., I got into a cab and left my mother on the front porch screaming my name. I had never heard her cry like that. She cried with such passion and hurt that it echoed throughout the neighborhood as I left. Although I knew I was hurting her, all I thought about was that she was trying to keep me stuck and that she did not understand my need for being with my church. Pastor Menard always said to watch family members and old friends who may try to keep you from serving God. With what I believed to be conviction in my heart, I left home believing my mom was my enemy and I was doing the right thing.

When I reflect now on that moment, quite frankly, it was just something about that scream that I could never shake in my mind. My mother's tears and screams on that day sounded like deep rooted wailing like I never heard before. The tears were truly coming from a place deep inside of her that I will never forget. It was a mother's helpless cry for her child.

Today, as I write this book, she has told me that she literally felt like I was leaving with Satan himself that morning. She shared with me that she did not know anything about Satan back then. She didn't even believe that there was a Satan. She told me, however, that somehow that morning when I left, she knew that he was real as she saw me ride off in the taxi-cab. She believed that I was being driven by evil forces and she was helpless in stopping them or me.

After I left that morning, I managed to travel with my three babies without much trouble. However, there were no words to describe how disillusioned I felt when I finally reached California. After several days on the bus with three babies, I was exhausted and ready to just lay my head down anywhere.

When I got there, I was not looking my best. As a matter of fact, I had an ugly gray coat on that I had previously purchased in Germany. I looked tired and I looked bad.

As a matter of fact, I felt ugly, disgusted and dirty in that coat. And the first thing my pastor said when he saw me was, "That's the ugliest coat I've ever seen."

I knew it was ugly, and I hated how wearing it made me feel. My family members at home didn't tell me just how awful that coat looked on me. I guess they were trying not to hurt my feelings.

Can you believe that I was so emotionally mixed up that I actually, used their reluctance to tell me the truth about my coat to mean that my family was not as truthful as my pastor? That was my way of thinking. This way of thinking was used to further justify why it was good that I left my biological family to be with my church family, and immediately I was convinced that the pastor was the only one who was going to always tell me the truth. I was hooked from that point on.

The pastor now took the place of my mother teacher, friend, father, leader, protector, and new pretend husband in my life. I was living in a fantasy, and I believed nobody loved me but the pastor. I thought nobody at the church had what I had, which was a secret relationship with my pastor. It was a secret and he made me feel like I was somebody in his life, on his team, and in God's sight.

And for years I remained "a somebody" in his life. I felt he treated me in special ways, and he paid particular attention to my kids and to my personal growth. Although I usually didn't have a lot of money, I had everything else that I needed with this family group, and I never asked my biological family for anything except Christmas toys once a year.

In my mind, I was self- sufficient, as long as I had my church. In fact, that was one of the teachings of the church. We were to never lie to the Pastor and we were to always keep things in the "family." The pastor promised all of us a better life. The only thing I had to do in order to keep this new life was to always remember that my husband was a deadbeat dad who didn't love me. This was drilled into my head from the moment I arrived. Also, I had to remember that my mother did not deserve respect above the pastor since she didn't protect me against sexual abuse when

I was a child. This was drilled in my head. Lastly, anyone outside our church family were not my friends until the pastor approved of them. He constantly reminded me of these points over and over again whenever I showed signs of being homesick.

Those rules were simple, right? So, for the next 10 years I was conditioned to only tell the pastor my inner thoughts. I was conditioned to believe he was the only one who could help raise my children. You see, he and the other church members constantly told each other that we were not good parents without the pastor in our lives. I was conditioned to believe that Jesus would only speak to the pastor concerning my spiritual needs and that any other pastor was not approved by God to counsel me. Also, I was not spiritual enough to hear from God myself, so I was conditioned to always tell the pastor things that I thought I heard from God. He would interpret them for me.

I was conditioned to believe that I was mentally ill without his ministry and that God placed me with his ministry because something was wrong with me and my kids. I was conditioned to believe that if I ever left his church, something bad would happen to me or my kids. I was conditioned to believe that everything the pastor was giving us was because God sent him to us and that my personal belongings belonged to him because he was taking care of me and my kids. I was conditioned to believe that having contact with my husband without the pastor knowing meant that I was being disloyal to him, and I was certainly deceived by the devil.

One of the things I never wanted to be called was a dumb woman. This is what he called me when I showed signs of longing for my family or my husband, the father of my kids. I hated being called that because he would make an open spectacle of me in front of the other women. I was shamed and shunned whenever it looked like I was looking for love and support from my biological family. I was taught that being a strong woman meant that I did not need a man to help me and I didn't need love from anyone outside of our church family. That was unnecessary. We were self-contained.

I was conditioned to believe that my kids were mentally ill and the Pastor being in their lives was the only thing keeping them stable.

I was conditioned to believe that anyone who spoke against our church was the devil, which included the bishop, the church across town, the former members who left the church, my mother, and any of my relatives. I was rewarded with favor from my new family if I was friends with those who were friends with my pastor. And I was conditioned to believe that anyone who disrespected the pastor was an enemy to the whole team.

As I got accustomed to the norms of the church family, slowly I began to see the other reason why Pastor Menard was not able to help my husband change anymore.

While in Germany, my husband stopped giving the pastor the proper respect. This is what destroyed their relationship. My husband refused to follow the pastor's instructions. I guess in Pastor Menard's eyes, my husband was disrespectful. It didn't help the situation when Pastor Menard found out that my husband was against me being there in California.

Because of the lack of submission to the pastor, my husband was an enemy of the church. It began to make sense that if I was going to be a member of this church, I was never to have contact with my husband until he showed respect to the pastor, the man of God. I was convinced that I could never confide in my husband and that, somehow, I would be in trouble with the pastor and God if I did.

As time went on, I began to resent my husband more and more, and I did not accept his position in my life. In a word, I was becoming more and more self-righteous and judgmental.

With my mind made up, the kids and I stayed in California with the church for almost seven years. A few more members joined the church there, but only I and one other female, along with the pastor and his wife, were a part of the original church from Germany.

At the church I noticed that I was not the only single woman with children. Other women had split up with their spouses too. Pastor Menard never told any of us as single women to leave our husbands. He just constantly reminded us of how unmanly and weak our husbands were. Whenever there was a phone call from any of our husbands, the pastor would coach us on how we should talk to them. He would even give us the words to say. Before long, I was cold as ice to my husband and never spoke to him without the pastor's presence. By being in the background, Pastor Menard said he was protecting us from being "dumb women" who could be deceived by our spouses. He was going to teach us how to be independent, self-sufficient women. He said that it was his ministry to help single women become strong, respectable females. Interestingly, a lot of the families who joined our church seemed to either have marital problems that lead to eventual break-ups or the new families would suddenly just quit the church. It was all so weird, but I couldn't see what was happening.

Let me sum up what happened in my life up to this point…

After just three years of marriage, I left my husband in Germany and eventually went to California to join the church when it relocated there. It was a hard decision at first, but when Pastor Menard told me what would happen to my kids and me, I made the hardest decision of my life because of fear.

Besides, the pastor presented a good life to me. He made sure that the church members helped me with the kids. He said that I would be able to follow my dreams and that I would be saved by sticking with him.

So, like Eve in the Garden of Eden, I took the "fruit." I "swallowed the pill." I "ate the poison." I "took the bait." I "ate from the tree that God said don't eat from." I became an adulterer and took my family into a life of sin! (Gen 3)

Chapter 4
Did You Mean to Destroy My Life?

Please allow me to explain a very important concept before moving along. These days, it seems that being an adulterer is in vogue. It's like the thing to do. A lot of people would say that I'm too uptight in thinking that being an adulterer is a bad thing. Today, it seems everyone is doing it and we feel justified.

I met a woman who told me that black women have been treated badly for so long that we now are doing what we have to do. As a race of women, we have bounced back and now we are letting men know that we don't need them. We'll do whatever it takes to provide for our kids, keep our self-worth and move on with our lives, even if it means pickin' up another man on the side or using men to get what we want. It's like we are paying them back for what they have done to us for so long. That seems to be the way of the day. I get it. It's survival with a little revenge attached to it.

A lot of women feel that being an adulterer or just giving a man a taste of his own medicine seems to be long overdue. Many women, despite their nationality, seem to just be tired of being hurt, being taken for granted, and being abandoned by men who have been getting away with these same things for years! Enough is enough! Women are making the playing field equal these days, and I get that.

Although I understand that many women are tired of being hurt, being taken for granted, and being abandoned, I do not agree that adultery is the answer. Adultery not only hurts the spouse that is being cheated on, but it also negatively effects the one who is the adulterer. As a matter of fact, for a Christian who is really following Christ (and not simply attending church), sin is not the answer to getting revenge. We have taken matters into our own hands when it comes to handling men and now things are worse. Divorce, fornication, hatred, and strife are so common-place that there are countless numbers of children without fathers and even full-time mothers. And to make matters worse, a great number of women are so bitter that there seems to be a new generation of youth who are heartless and numb to the feelings of others. As one man put it, there seems to be a new generation of children being born today with no souls. Whew! I don't know about you, but that's scary. Granted, there are many, many causes for this type of phenomenon, but the questions that must be answered within each of us as Christians are, "Am I a part of the solution or part of the problem?" "How does God feel about the way I am handling my life today?" "Whose side am I on; God's side, or my own side?"

Here are other questions. Am I doing this the way that God wants me to handle things? Is there a better way?

Being an adulterer is not a fad or a badge of honor. Personally, it made me spiritually sick and spiritually deformed from that point on. For example, in order to justify adultery (which I did), I had to justify lying. I had to also justify fornication. I had to justify deception, hatred and jealousy. All of those acts of the flesh go together in order to live a lifestyle in adultery. I became a liar. Again, these days it seems that being a liar is not so bad either. Everybody does it every now and then. It's one of those sins that most of us just tolerate. There are those in the world who could present a good argument for telling lies. Just look around you. Most of us tell lies to each other like it's just a part of survival.

But here's the real deal. Lying to others led me to lying to myself, or was it vice versa? Some would say that I started lying to myself first and then that led to lying to others. I guess that's similar to the question: what came first, the chicken or the egg? In my opinion, it doesn't matter at this point which came first.

In the sight of God, all liars are an abomination to Him whether we are lying to ourselves or to others. A liar is not what God is calling us to be. It is true that the intent of our heart is what really matters to God when we find ourselves having to tell a lie. That again, is not the point. Being an adulterer, thief, or murderer in order to carry out our own fleshly desires is never okay with God. Take it from me, I learned that the hard way.

That's the worst thing you can do to yourself. Lie to yourself and you will live in a private hell for the rest of your life. The devil loves when you lie to yourself - then he can have you on remote control. He does not have to worry about you defecting from his control because you're in his prison. That's where I was. I was in a prison cell that, over time, I created for myself. After a while the enemy didn't worry about me too much. I would just regulate myself. It's like a drug addict that self-administers the product. The dealer doesn't have to find the addict; the addict will find the dealer and keep himself intoxicated. That's how it was for me. It became easy for the devil to lure me into other sins, slowly and methodically. Here's the wicked part: I felt righteous. I was fooled by self-righteousness, self-deception and off I went living in a world of my own where Jesus became nothing more than a Bible character. There were times in my journey where I even began to question whether salvation was even real or necessary. Everything, as time went on, seemed like make-believe. Alice in Wonderland!

After I committed adultery, my whole way of thinking changed. I was under the impression that having sex with a married man was the will of God. Despite what the Bible clearly said, adultery meant something different for me than it did for the rest of the world. The truth is, I was like Alice in Wonderland who went down the rabbit hole. To this day, I still have trouble looking at that movie. Better yet, I was Dorothy in the *Wizard of Oz* who just left the real world and suddenly found herself in a foreign land after a tornado. To top it all off, it wasn't long after that I received divorce papers in the mail. My husband divorced me.

Everything in my life from that point on became redefined. What was once right was now wrong. What was once wrong was now alright in my new life. My identity was being redefined for me. The funny thing about it was that I was taught well in the Scriptures while attending this church.

However, I also learned that knowing Scriptures and living out the Scriptures are two different things. When we only *know* the scripture without *living* it out, we are doing what Satan does. He knows the Word of God but will not follow it. How was I any different than those we call sinners when I refused to follow what I was reading and teaching? I don't know about you, but that's scary. Preaching, teaching, quoting, but not living the Scriptures made me a hypocrite, and later on in my life that bothered me. Living like that was making me into a two-faced monster.

Pastor Menard, on the other hand, didn't seem to have a problem with living two lives. The pastor was very smart when it came to explaining, or expounding on the Scriptures, but it took me a long time to see that "applying the Scriptures" was only for us who attended his church, never for him. He was considered special and didn't have to show that he followed the Scriptures to the extent that the rest of us did. Because I trusted him though, I believed and accepted that fact for many years to come. For the most part, it seemed he was exempt from actually living the Scriptures. All he had to do as the pastor was to know the Scriptures so that we could follow them.

Being honest with myself now, I came to grips with the fact that I really believed him because I wanted to live my life free to have this secret relationship with him and be saved at the same time. He told me what I wanted to hear. And I loved listening to him for that reason. Being an adulterer was making a statement in my life -somebody wants me, somebody loves me! I was done wrong and now I get to have revenge.

Without much resistance, I believed everything Pastor Menard said. My thinking was that I was special to God because God allowed me to have this relationship and be saved at the same time. I just knew I was saved because I didn't smoke, drink, curse, or lie to my pastor (the man of God). I thought that it was ok to lie to my family because they were sinners and they didn't know God like I knew God. I was special, at least that's how I felt. Seriously folks, my way of thinking was being reconditioned! Whatever I was taught in kindergarten was now being relearned under a new understanding. In kindergarten, I learned to treat people the way I wanted to be treated. Now, I was learning to treat only the Christians in our special group the way I wanted to be treated. More specifically, those people who were in our organization, in our small church and in our club, and especially the ones that respected our pastor were given special treatment. As I search the Scriptures today, I understand that the Bible calls this "respect of persons" and God hates this. But all of this seemed okay to me back then because I was getting something in return - acceptance and belonging.

It seems that in California I spent time learning "how to be saved" according to man. Pastor Menard was teaching the Bible in church, but the application of the Scriptures was coming across a different way behind closed doors. I was slowly getting used to praising God for His Word and "having a good time in church," and at the same time, following another set of rules when I was alone with Pastor Menard. I was getting used to it, while at the same time, not thinking that I was sinning. I had a "special" faith. And now I know that that kind of faith leads to death.

"The thief's purpose is to steal and kill and destroy. My purpose is to give them a rich and satisfying life" —John 10:10, NLT

They don't like US

We spent several years in California, and then the whole church moved again. This time we moved to Kentucky. Before relocating, things were difficult there, but I received my Associate's degree at one of the local colleges, lived in my own home and learned to care for my children with little help from my family. I didn't have much work experience because I did volunteer work at the church. Because of this, the pastor became a bigger influence in my children's lives. We were at the church almost every day. He was teaching me how to be a better mother and teaching my kids how to be better kids. They were still rather young, and we had little contact with our biological families, so Pastor Menard was the only father-figure they knew.

Under the direction of the pastor, I kept my children from contacting their real dad. Although their dad tried to contact them once he found out where we were, the kids did not know him. They only knew what the pastor and I shared about him, which was often negative. As previously mentioned, whenever their dad tried to reach out to any of us, we had to be in the presence of the pastor. Pastor Menard always regulated the phone calls and would ask questions after we hung up. It was so very stressful to talk on the phone or even to receive mail from their dad (my ex-husband). Everything was screened. Also, the questions were grueling and frequently done in public (in front of the other church members). So, a lot of times, you felt like the spotlight was on you every time you got a call, a letter or a gift from a biological family member. Back then I guessed that Pastor Menard wanted to make sure none of us were being persuaded away from the "truth" by our family members. Pastor Menard did this because he said we (women and children) needed protecting and he felt that he was the only one taking care of the children now. "Nobody deserves to speak to your kids without my knowledge, especially since I'm the one taking care of them!" he said. The pastor constantly reminded me that my ex-husband didn't want me and that he was not interested in reconciliation. He would say, "If your ex-husband really wanted his family, he would be here to confront me (Pastor Menard)!"

Although, my ex-husband sent child support and letters, he never did show up, and the only explanation I had for this was what Pastor Menard told me. I truly believed that my husband didn't want me or his kids. Having that engrained in my mind, I continued to be hard-hearted and lived in resentment and feelings of rejection for a long time. As far as I knew, I was rejected by the person who was supposed to love me.

Therefore, when I was pressured to be cold and rude to him, I felt ok with it. But it was mainly because of the scolding I and my kids would receive from Pastor Menard after each call. Although it hurt, it seemed that keeping a distance from my ex-husband and biological family was the best thing. I never informed my ex-husband of any changes about the children. I never included him in any decisions. I totally removed him from my kids' lives and tried to replace my kids' dad with the pastor. In doing so, I became totally bitter, not just toward my ex-husband, but toward all men. Because Pastor Menard talked about the husbands of the other women too, I just got this impression that most men were weak, and they didn't care about their families or marriages. Soon, my ex just stopped calling altogether. We never spoke again until almost 20 years later!

Now living under the guidance of the man of God, my kids and I got used to being in California as a family. We learned to live alone. Until one day, Pastor Menard said that we, as a whole church, needed to pack up and move. He told us that the move would be good for our morale. Since most of the church members were mainly from the mid-west states, we had group discussions about how great it would be to be closer to our home states. We could be closer to family. The pack up seemed a little odd since it was decided suddenly, but most of us welcomed the move.

After some months of planning, the whole church packed up one weekend and then hit the road to relocate to Kentucky. We were on the road for three days with most of the families from the church. (The names have been changed) Our caravan included the pastor and his wife with their two daughters (the Menards), the pastor's secretary (Sister Carrie), a sister (Sister Cheryl) and her son, another sister (Sis. Bruce) and her two children, a man and his pregnant wife (the Carsons), a different woman (Sis Tasha) and her two children, another man and wife with his three children (The Jakes) and my children and me. All in all, we were a group of about 21 people.

When we arrived in a small town in Kentucky after a very long road trip, the Carsons just disappeared in a matter of a few days; it was very weird.

They had gotten to Kentucky with the intention to stay, but a few days later, they took off without a word. We didn't hear from them again.

We had gotten used to people leaving the church like this, so not much was said. Our thought was they probably backslid and wanted to live in sin. Whenever families left our church, I just assumed that the families were out of the will of God.

However, the more perplexing and important thing at the time was the way we were treated when we arrived in this town.

The people there now seemed to follow us with their eyes. We drove into town as a church family - women, children, men, all the way from California. I guess it was very strange to them. However, it wasn't strange to us because we viewed ourselves as a Christian family who had all things in common. We felt empowered because we could rely on each other as a support.

We established residence and were met with stares and whispers from the local government offices. I guess it was a small town and everyone knew each other. The people in the offices appeared to be sensitive to new people moving in the area. When I met with social workers about my housing and welfare benefits, they would ask, "Oh, are you a part of that group of people who just moved here from California?" I would respond with yes. But I always wondered how weird it was for them to ask whether I was with a group. It was also weird that more than one case worker would ask me the same question. What was the big deal? I felt like a celebrity or somethin', but somehow, I didn't think these people were happy to see us. They would ask questions as to why we came and what we intended to do here.

I felt myself constantly explaining why I moved with my church to this area. What type of church is it, they asked? "Pentecostal," I would say. And then everything would be quiet -- an eerie silence would come that I could never put my finger on.

Later we learned that a church had been run out of town because the members handled snakes. We used to laugh at the audacity that we could be associated with a church that handled snakes! We did not handle snakes.

Nonetheless, we did not receive a very good welcome in Kentucky. Prejudice may have been a factor too -- we were mainly a black congregation. I was not sure whether we were singled out because we were a "black group" or a "church group ." I guess I'll never know. The relevance here is that a previous church was run out of town and so our church was on the radar. But why us?

What did we do so differently from the other churches in town? To me, I was just as normal as the next guy in town. I got enrolled with the local university, my children went to the local schools (later on I homeschooled them), I paid my rent and hung out with church friends. Why was I being targeted? Was it just me?

Regardless of how I felt, there was always a sense that *they don't like us here in this town*. But the rest of the church members and I continued to set up our homes, enroll in school, find jobs and live as a church family despite how uncomfortable it was. We didn't cause any trouble and were excited that everything was being reestablished in our lives, but still they didn't like us here, and I knew it. You might say, so why stay?

For the record, let me remind you that we left California as a group because we wanted to be closer to our biological families who lived in nearby states. We wanted to be able to visit with them more often; at least that's what we discussed as a church family before leaving for Kentucky. However, there was another reason we left California that only our pastor knew about. We as a church never discovered it until about seven years later.

The Club was Born

Like I said, most of us either found jobs or were enrolled in college as we began our lives in this new area. It was not easy. We were financially broke by the time we arrived. Therefore, many times we had to share our resources with each other. Anything we had (money, cars, houses, food or clothes, etc.) was divided between the families so that we all benefited. In the beginning, we had to live with each other until we found housing for each family. The pastor and his wife, however, had other family members there who helped them. They did not have to stay with us. As housing and jobs took time, we learned to put all of our resources together in order to live. We had to trust each other on new levels, and that was difficult. The pastor became the glue to making this happen. We did not trust each other, but we had something in common with each other. We all seemed to trust the pastor. Because of this, we all learned to depend on him as a father (just like the kids) to a greater degree.

Sometimes it was his money that fed us, paid the utility bills and provided a means to continue paying our personal bills until we had jobs to sustain ourselves. Each relationship was with the pastor and not necessarily with each other. He was the center for all of our needs. We learned to give our resources to him and then he would divide them in a way that benefited the whole team, not just one family. For example, if sister Bruce had $20 left in her bank account, she would give it to the pastor. He then would divide it so that all the families would have gas in their cars. It caught on, and that's how we lived, even down to the toilet paper. We made sure there was toilet paper for all, and none of us could be wasteful.

Meanwhile, the pastor slowly began to form a pastor support group with those of us who saw the benefit of sharing. We didn't mind giving our resources to the pastor because we believed that no one person was benefiting. He was able to provide for his family this way too. If his family needed something, he would take from what was collected in the group. It worked, and the arrangement is what got us through rough times.

Eventually income increased, but the system we used was still in place. It was working. Having that as a model, many of us were willing to continue using this plan, and it slowly became a way of life. Those of us willing to continue sharing and benefiting from each other's blessings kept doing it, and soon everyone bought in.

As time went on, we learned to depend on each other's finances, and soon we became the club. The club was comprised of a few church members who essentially were the inner circle for Pastor Menard. We had meetings outside of the church. The club acted as an elite group within the church because we were the main members who were faithful to the mission of the church and to the pastor. When the church opened to the public, the club was also opened to any new members joining the church. Although no one was refused membership with the church, each person who wanted to join the club had to be screened and accepted by Pastor Menard. There was no secret about our club, however we considered ourselves a family outside of church and our personal resources remained exclusively for the club members.

Although some of us missed the autonomy of having our own stuff, the whole concept of sharing was so powerful that we continued it even after we moved into our own homes. Some of the families went a step further by pairing up and moving in with each other. Living together cut down on costs and provided roommates for the single women. We lived together, went to church together and shared our resources together. And we continued giving a portion of our money to the pastor for his family. The money we gave was separate from our normal donations to the church. Each family kept what they needed to pay living expenses but gave the rest either to the church, club fund or ultimately, to the pastor for his family.

This worked well until there were suspicions and mismanagement of funds by certain members. To keep honesty and order in the club, the pastor came up with the idea of creating rank order for individuals.

Consequently, the members of the club were broken up in ranks based on their loyalty to the club and the number of years they were a part of the church. If you were faithful to the church, that faithfulness was demonstrated *by the number of years* you stayed with the church without abandoning it. You were considered a lifetime member. And the level of loyalty you had *for the team* was the other factor. Your loyalty to the team was based on what the pastor thought about you. It was subjective.

It was similar to having military rank or a class system. There was a level for the executives. These were the ones who showed more loyalty to the club, had the greatest number of years with the church, and possessed the most professional skills out of the whole team.

The second and third levels were called the cabinet and staff levels. These were the ones who showed loyalty to the church and club but had less years in the church and were not as professional in business as the top level. The last level was for those that the pastor did not trust as much but who showed some commitment by staying with the church for a few years. Also, they were not as savvy in business as the other members. It was on this level that people spent time proving themselves to the pastor and other club members.

The rank structure brought about order and control in the club so that people would not disrespect each other. The ranks also kept us separate from each other psychologically. For example, those of us on the top level thought we were better than those on the other levels. At times, we conducted ourselves as such. If a person on a lower rank had a disagreement or different opinion than a person on a higher level, then the lower ranked person knew to give in because of his/her "place" or rank in the club. This kept everyone doing the "right" thing. The head of the club was the pastor.

His wishes were acted out through those rank levels depending on what it was. If his wish was of an urgent matter, the higher-ranking person would relay the pastor's wishes to the team and others would follow. If the matter was less important, then the lower rank would handle it. For example, all major financial matters were carried out by higher ranking people. And any cooking for the group or manual labor that needed to be done in the yard, those tasks were mainly handled by the lower ranking individuals and the kids. There was overlap between the duties of each level, but for the most part everyone knew where they stood in the mind of the pastor based on their rank. Depending on a person's behavior, many people bounced back and forth on these levels at various times. I eventually earned my way to the executive level and stayed there.

The caste system that is prominent in some cultures would be a great example of this arrangement. Just like real society, eventually our club system turned out to be about the "haves" and "have nots." If you were on the higher levels, you had more and were expected to have more money and social influence within the group. Those on the lower levels didn't have much money, nor were they called in to make the major decisions. They acted as the workers who carried out the decisions of the executive level. It was like we all lived in this separate world that was created by Pastor Menard.

This rank system worked well unless a person said, "No," to Pastor Menard's request. If a person did not want to carry out the pastor's wishes, there was a club meeting that put that person in the spotlight. We always had meetings to solve issues or discuss our plans.

In the beginning, being in the club was a true social and financial benefit. It was our way of being self-sufficient in a community that did not seem to like us much. We learned to work together and help each other to achieve personal goals as well as the goals of the church. The club was there early at church, never missed services and there late at night. The club carried the bulk of church's finances because we were the ones who cared most about our church, and it was the club's responsibility to see it be successful.

As a matter of fact, the mission of the club in the beginning was about working as a team to become financially and socially stable so that we could benefit the work of the Lord. Everyone was to support each other as we got our degrees, bought property and built the church. There were even some Christian business/ministry ideas that we were trying to finance as well. We had many ideas.

There were some other advantages too. We met together and socialized on the weekends. The club was enjoyable because we took extravagant trips, ate expensive meals, went on spending sprees and vacations. And we even paid each other's bills as necessary. If you were in the club, you never had to worry about anything. We all shared our food, so no one ever went hungry.

Something, however, changed along the way. The direction of the club seemed to take a turn, and Pastor Menard seemed to be increasingly frustrated with the group. When members seemed happy about giving and receiving things in the club, Pastor Menard seemed to have looks of anger. He would make statements as if the club was not giving enough to him. He began to count how much he gave as opposed to how much others were giving. Suddenly there were meetings to discuss how the club could benefit Pastor Menard more since he was doing a lot of work being the father of the group. He should be cared for more since he gave the most by fathering the members. Then one day, he announced that the club was his club and his secretary began saying that those of us in it should be making sure he is taken care of first.

Anyone who didn't agree to that could leave. Everyone was silent. Here's the problem with leaving. By the time the pastor began wanting more from the club, most of us had already given all that we had. We had maxed out our giving and were sustaining our families with those sacrifices. We, as a group, were already so intertwined with each other; nothing belonged to just one person and there was nothing extra to give. In order to increase our care for the pastor, it would mean that we would have to give more, even from our own retirement funds, family savings, insurance policies, home loans, school loans, and any future money or resources. This made the morale of the club more and more grim. We had a debt that we could not pay.

Gradually, the club became the means by which we were to pay back the time, money, resources, or stuff that the pastor had given to us. He was not asking the church to pay because the church operated separately from the club. Besides, he as a pastor would never demand repayment for doing the work of God. This was the club, and the club was different from the church (on a case by case situation). We all belonged to the church, but the whole church did not belong to the club. For example, Sis. Menard was not a club member. She just benefited from the club's resources because she was the First Lady and the pastor's wife.

Without at least trying to pay him back, it looked like we were just using him. It looked like we were taking advantage of his kindness when he was helping our families. As a dedicated father, he was giving speeches and lectures to our kids more than the average pastor would do. He was buying things in our homes when we didn't have furniture, and he counseled and coached the club members more than the average church member. How could we pay him back? The truth was that there was not a price that we could come up with that could satisfy what we owed, and we didn't have the money to pay anyway. He didn't know an amount that we owed him and neither did we. He was not only asking for the money he put in but the value of the services he was providing. How much was that? He was helping us to raise our kids and treating us like his very own children. How much does that cost? Regardless of the amount, he and his secretary suddenly became debt collectors.

As a matter of fact, we all became debt collectors at various times; however, his secretary was the one who mainly ensured that the pastor was compensated. The pressure of owing him stung and lingered in almost every situation and conversation. There was a "you owe me" mindset that hovered over the club, and the bill we owed kept rising. We even came up with a price that the club may have owed the pastor for all the help and financial assistance he gave, but when we were close to paying it off, something else was tacked on. He would pay for things or buy things for the club and then say that the club owed him the money back. These were things we needed and a few other things we could have done without. It was his club now, so he could buy what he wanted, and we had to pay the bill. No matter how much we tried to pay the debts as a group, he would complain that he never felt the benefits of being in the club like he intended it to be. He said we were benefiting more than he.

Every so often, he would explain that the club was originally designed to benefit him and his family financially and then it was to help the other members. He explained that it started because of him trying to take care of us, and now we should be taking care of him. This speech made me feel guilty and ashamed that I would allow myself to neglect the man of God. I was not the only one who felt this way. Ironically, we all looked like kids who had been staying in their momma's house without paying rent. The Scriptures taught that we should have been taking care of the man of God. There was a different flavor in the group now. Sis. Carrie, the pastor's secretary, acted as the spokesperson and bill collector for the pastor. Sis. Carrie, like a drill sergeant, began to demand that we as a club pay our debt to the Pastor with interest. After all, he was the one taking care of us and our kids, it was only fair. How do you resist that? All of the families received so much counseling, instruction, protection and correction from the man of God that to not give back was just dirty and unchristian. After this turnaround, our number one obligation was to make sure the pastor was paid and that he felt appreciated for all the labor he did for the team and church.

Pastor Menard still spoke about the other goals of the club, but he made it clear that he had to be paid first. We club members could continue to enjoy expensive dinners, fun activities, rent-free shelter, paid bills, car repairs, protection, and a sense of family, but for a fee. Now all of that was done at the direction of the pastor and for a fee that was to be determined by his secretary.

On one hand, it wasn't such a bad idea because club members also enjoyed going out to eat, going on expensive trips and participating in plans for owning houses and land. It still seemed to be a good idea for securing our futures. The only problem was that in exchange for these luxuries, members had to pay outrageous prices or give up their rights to their personal lives. The pastor didn't mind forgiving our debt if we then would allow him access to our resources without question. For example, if all you had was a hundred dollars, he would let you keep that to pay your bills, but you still owed him and you must be willing to give the pastor your bank account information or whatever so that he could be compensated.

Since none of us were able to fully repay Pastor Menard for all the help he gave us, we lived out the rest of the time indebted to him. And because of this indebtedness, we became not only his spiritual children in the Lord, but also his servants.

To put it plainly, as a club member, your club membership was literally exchanged for servanthood, and because the pastor was also your spiritual father, your adulthood was changed into childhood, literally. As adult people we practically assumed the role of children even though most of us were reaching between 30- 50 years old. He felt justified in shaking, pulling and slapping the women, shaking and spanking the kids, yelling at and publicly reprimanding the men, and owning any of our possessions in our homes, bank accounts or retirement funds.

Some years later, when I became employed outside the church, it was weird that I actually would go home from work having to live a like a child while in a grown-up body. I guess you could say I had two lives! At work I was an adult woman working a full-time job, but at home I was a grown- up child living under the rules of the club that were governed by our pastor. Whenever I got out of line while at home, I was punished either psychologically or physically (slapped across my face).

In each of those lives I was under a different mindset and literally governed by two different influences, fear and more fear. Afraid to tell someone at work for fear of being disloyal and ungrateful for the club, and at the same time afraid of making the pastor angry and having to pay the consequences. Looking at it now, it seems that I was living under self-deception, thinking I was living for Christ while still fulfilling the works of the flesh. I was calling that lifestyle godly. That was not godly! I know that now. It was religious living. I was religious, and I was in bondage - living two lives!

In essence, I sold my soul to the club and the pastor had complete control over my life. He was happy, and I was happy that he was happy. What I got in return was a life where I didn't have to worry about paying the electric bill and other stuff. Someone in the club handled the bills. I didn't worry about paying rent. Someone else handled that since most of us began living together under one roof. This allowed us to cut costs. I never had to worry about being stranded at night; there was always someone in the club who would rescue me or change my flat tire. I had all of this security, but the truth was it came with a price that I didn't want to pay, a price I couldn't pay. My personal life, including my desires, goals, and God-given destiny had to be squashed - destroyed - in order to have the security I had. Truthfully, I had to become someone else in order to keep both worlds. It's embarrassing to say that I didn't really know who I was.

I lived a life of false security. It was false because the security was based on me being in servitude to one man who could take almost everything away from me with just one gesture to this staff. I felt cared for, but owned nothing. I guess you could say I was a rich slave!

Anything I had belonged to the club, and I was never safe if I was completely being myself. I'm not saying I wanted to be wild, disrespectful, or unfaithful. I just wanted to be in a relationship or environment where I didn't have feel like I had to lie all the time. Secretly, I began to hate my life.

I could not tell the whole truth and still enjoy what I had. I had to tell half-truths to be able to keep what I had. If security is based on a lie, then that's not security. That's a form of security, but not full security, which makes it false. If it's not able to stand in the face of truth, it's not true security. Anything that can crumble in the face of truth is false. I learned that the hard way.

In the club, we often said we were free, but in reality, if we disrespected the pastor (whether intentionally or not), we had our items and club privileges revoked just like prisoners. Things could be taken away at a whim. If he just thought you were unfaithful, then you were unfaithful until you proved your innocence. And until then, you were shunned by the group. Watching the flow of things, it seemed that all I had to do was worship our leader and I would receive extra benefits.

Look, we never said to each other, "Hey let's worship the pastor!" No one would dare say such a thing out loud. It's just that if you did worship him, life was so much easier. If you made the leader look good in public, we would actually get paid. It wasn't real money at first, but it was token money. Pastor Menard designed a payment system to reward those who were especially diligent in making him as the leader look good. If you were instrumental in making the pastor feel good and own more stuff, like a Mercedes 500 SEL, there were rewards and favor.

As a matter of fact, our pastor had two Mercedes and a big beautiful house.

It was hard to swallow the change of the club at first, but one person would go along with it and soon the rest of us would join in too. Despite how I felt in the end, the main reason I was willing to be a full participant in the club was because I believed that he was hearing from God and I was the one who was sinning against God by not taking care of the man of God. We were his responsibility in the sight of God, but he was our responsibility in the sight of God too. There was a relationship between him and us. It was hard for me to believe that Pastor Menard was anything but a man of God. He had some strange ways, but I believed he was anointed by God. He could really preach and teach!

The rest of the club members and I seemed willing to do whatever it took to please our leader and promote our club. The glitter of feeling rich when we went to stores (we could get almost everything we wanted with the club credit cards, as long as you were in good standing with the pastor and had the proper rank) kept me engaged with the club (the club cards were our personal credit cards that we turned in to the group).

All this worked for me for several years. For a time, I enjoyed being in the club and having a sense of belonging. However, in order to continue with the joys of the club, I fell deeper and deeper in debt and it seemed that I never got ahead. For example, if I received an increase in pay on my job, I couldn't pay off my bills without first checking with the group. No one could do anything that could be a financial hardship to the rest of the members. As a member, I had to contribute to numerous unexpected bills that were made for the club in addition to my personal finances. Financially things were out of control. Also, if I was buying clothes for myself, I had to make sure that others in the club didn't feel I was getting too much. Others operated the same.

To my frustration, after years of service and time to the club, we were still broke. We all seemed to have the same old clothes and same old cars. There was never enough money for any of us to really advance. Financially, there was a continuous strain and no real change. We kept spending money on shopping sprees, but most of them were increasingly being spent on Pastor Menard. The pressure of this lifestyle may have been taking a toll on me little by little.

Pastor Menard used to say, "Nobody is being forced to do anything." I agreed that no one was forced to stay. But when I saw members try to leave, I noticed that there was a lot of anger and what seemed to be retaliation. After a while I wondered privately whether a person really was free to leave.

Anyone who tried to get out of the club was shunned in the club and at church and even at their own homes. Remember, some of us were roommates so there was never a place to go where a club member wasn't there. A person threatening to leave was portrayed as a traitor, and it seemed that very quickly his privileges would disappear until he complied with the rest of the group. They were suddenly enemies of the pastor, and we all had to treat that person in a certain way. Leave? You're asking why didn't I just leave? Where was I going to go? The door had already been shut between my family and me. The only friends I had (all the time) were the club members. And still there was one more issue that kept me living this life. I was addicted to selfish ambition. Eventually, Pastor Menard made me think I was his number one girl. After proving myself, I was promoted and allowed to manage the team and business affairs while wearing several different titles. I was addicted to titles too. Within our club family, I had prestige. I became the club secretary and Sis. Carrie remained his personal secretary.

It seemed that the club always had meetings but the meetings that all of us dreaded the most were the meetings in black.

"Club meetings in black" were the worst kinds of meetings because they were the ones where we all dressed in black and discussed the "bad behavior" of a club member. As with most things in our club, dressing in black didn't start out being a bad thing. Club meetings in black used to symbolize success and a time for planning our financial investments. But as time went on, a meeting in black meant trouble. As a member, you never wanted to be the discussion or topic of the agenda for a meeting dressed in black.

Only the real serious situations were discussed in black. The most serious thing a person could do was disrespect the pastor. Also, a meeting in black was called to discuss the finances and ways to generate money. There could be a meeting in black in situations where someone on a lower rank didn't take the suggestion of someone on an upper rank. Let's say someone on the executive level requested for the person on a lower level to get an extra job to pay some additional bills. If the lower level member did not want to carry out the request of the higher ranked person, there was a meeting in black for not showing esprit de corps. Esprit de corps was showing teamwork towards the club. Not being willing to support or sacrifice for the club was grounds for a meeting in black with your name on it.

If you held back money from the pastor or group, there was a meeting in black. If you spoke up about a matter that you disagreed with and it sounded as if you disagreed with the head or made the pastor look bad in public, there was a meeting in black. If you disagreed with any rule of the club that the pastor instituted, then there was a meeting in black. Just having the threat of a meeting in black kept most of us carrying out the wishes of each other but mostly the wishes of the pastor.

We all dressed in black and sat around the table for hours (sometimes days) talking about the person's behavior. The questions were grueling, and usually the person was crying after so many hours of emotional and psychological distress. There were punishments and sanctions given to the person that would last for months depending on the offense. If you didn't have the favor of the pastor, he and the rest of the group were unmerciful to you. It seemed like a psychological beat down in order get compliance. It was very intense.

As a member, your house became the club's house. Your personal time became the club's time. Your personal mission became the club's mission. Your car or credit card belonged to the club. Your savings became the club's savings. Your personal items (i.e. cellphone, television, furniture, 401k, or income tax check) became the club's property. On our insurance policies, we removed our children and spouses as beneficiaries and put the pastor's name or a club member's name on it. There were few marriages. And some marriages were either denied, approved, or arranged by the pastor. Any hesitation, any refusal, any unwillingness would mainly result in either reprimand, humiliation, or emotional punishment. Like I said, at first giving up these things for the benefit of the whole group was not bad since we all benefited. However, the changes that occurred later made giving these things up grievous to me. And it was no longer a request; it was an obligation and burden. My willingness to support the man of God caused me to find some reward in it, but sometimes I just wanted out. But how do you say I don't want to support the pastor after everything he has done for me and my family? So, I found some peace with staying in it.

He's our Father

On occasions, the pastor felt quite comfortable slapping us women across the face if we were disrespectful to him or if we disobeyed his instruction. The slapping was usually followed by demotion from your rank and extra sanctions. We often said during the club meetings that everyone was free to leave if we disagreed with how we were being treated or did not want to give their personal items, but (the truth was) if you exercised that right, there would be swift and certain punishment. The number one punishment was shunning and then public ridicule of how you are unfaithful to the family. You might even have to pay back all the money that you used while in the club. Nobody had the money for that. And the shunning (where you and sometimes your kids were ignored by the whole group) was too much to bear. You were not free!

Every now and then, someone would show hesitation to following the club rules and Pastor Menard would quickly address it. If any of us felt that we were uncomfortable with the new arrangement, he would act concerned by talking to us privately to get us to say what we really felt. In the private meetings, you were made to feel that he understood your concerns and he was going to make changes for the better. Days later however, he would bring up the private conversation in front of the whole group, and when it was presented, you would appear as a traitor. Everyone had their turn being the one in the spotlight. Just like me, we all quickly learned to either keep our true feelings inside or be prepared to look like the one who doesn't care about the man of God. The other alternative was to simply decide to like the new changes, support them and find a way to live with them. Leaving was hardly an option since many of us had nowhere to go. It seemed that the fact that the majority of us came from broken relationships was a major factor.

I decided to live with the rules thinking that God was really in agreement with this. I had some doubts, but I learned early on to second guess myself. Besides, acting on my doubts caused me, on several occasions, to be presented to the group as a lunatic. I was then shunned and humiliated in front of the group, being called "psychotic," and sometimes I was slapped across the face.

I was hit across the face on a number of occasions, sometimes in front of my kids and other times in front of other club members.

One day, for example, I questioned Pastor Menard privately about whether he was having sexual relationships with the other women. He always told me that if I asked him things privately then he would respond privately. So, I asked him about the other women. Although we personally had stopped talking about our relationship for several months, I thought that he and I still had a special relationship and I felt that I could ask him. It became odd to me that a lot of the women all seemed to have a type of fear of him. They were very timid and seemed to be fixed on trying to please him at any cost. I thought they were being hit like I was. I became suspicious. What was their obsession in pleasing the pastor? It looked weird; maybe they were his girlfriends too. None of the women ever said it out loud, but there were traces of sexual encounters (i.e. smells, closed doors, funny looks, fixing up of clothes, hurried movements in the office while the doors were closed, jealousies among the women, and secrets, lots and lots of secrets).

I tried to confront him about my suspicions and was immediately yelled at, thrown out of his office, and even pushed and slapped. He made a public scene and began calling me crazy or "psychotic" (as he put it). He made me out to be a crazed woman who was out of control. Everyone looked at me in shame as if I had just blasphemed. This happened more than one time. And having to experience that made me (and I suspect the other women too) stay quiet about his "special relationships." I have seen him do this to other women too. They were yelled at and kicked out of his office. They were called "psychotic," but I never knew what the screaming was for. All I knew was that the sister appeared to be crying and sometimes I heard the commotion in the other room as if there was a fight. Unfortunately, all of the kids observed their mothers being slapped a few times. If the children tried to help their moms, they would be shunned or spanked too.

I figured out that the women, like me, had been strung along, waiting to marry him too. To make matters worse, he would say that, "We are all grown, and grown- ups can have sex with whoever they wanted as long as it was consenting." Yes, we were grown when it came to having sex, but it appeared that in his mind we were his kids when dealing with him about anything else. We were subordinate.

When it came to anything else, we were treated like children all the way down to being punished in front our kids. I had my church keys yanked away from me and my titles stripped at various times throughout my time within the club and church. It was mainly because he said I was disrespectful. I answered him in the wrong tone of voice, I questioned him about a decision he made, or I was accused of lying to him about something. I remember being hit so hard across the face that I could see white lights in my eye for months. The blood vessels were broken, it swelled and turned black and blue. I had been slapped before but never where there was a lasting bruise. It was embarrassing to tell my daughter a lie to cover up what really happened.

The next day when he realized what he had done, he told me that I should not let the first lady know, because she would see that I did something wrong. It was my fault. So, I stayed away from her and just wore make up to cover it up. Soon after that, he didn't slap me as much as he slapped the others. But prior to that incident, the slapping, the scolding, the yelling, the pulling, the public humiliation, and calling me names ("dumb woman," "psychotic," " fat," "sick," "psycho") went on for years.

After the episodes, he would treat me normally until there was another outburst. Sometimes I would get slapped because he was angry with one of the other women. I was the scape goat for many years. Whenever they made him upset, it would start out as a reprimand to them and then it would turn into a lashing out at me. He made me responsible for the other women's conduct. If they didn't do something right, I was pushed in the forehead or grabbed by the collar, pushed or grabbed by the shoulders and shaken up until they pleased him. A lot of times it was better that I just do whatever the assignment was so that he would stop screaming and hitting. Sometimes I thought that the sisters did things on purpose to make him angry just so that they could see me get knocked around.

As time went on though, he began to publicly (in front of the club members) hit the women too. And I no longer took the hits for the other women. Maybe it was because I begged him to stop using me as the go to person. Seeing the other women being slapped, though was worse than it happening to me. They were hit more frequently, and sometimes the women would not give in and just agree with him. You see, the sessions would last for hours on end. He would be yelling and asking questions, demanding them to see whatever his point of view was. There was crying and hours of interrogation while all the club members looked on. Whenever these situations happened, every club member knew not to talk or engage with the one on the spot.

I lived in fear every single day. Even when the pastor was not around, I lived in fear, intense fear. It didn't matter if I messed up or not, I knew I could be slapped across the face for someone else's failures at the next club meeting or gathering. My self-esteem withered away, and I felt like a prisoner in my own church, house, club, and life. I would go to church shaking on the inside, hoping that we could get through a day where there was no hitting or failures. I worked with the staff trying to make sure they didn't make mistakes, so I would do my work and theirs too, just to keep peace. I would cry alone at night thinking that this was how things were supposed to be because I had no other family.

One very vivid memory I'll never forget is when the club members were getting reprimanded one day by the pastor because something came up missing. Everyone was stressed out looking for whatever it was. All I remember was that I was crawling on the floor with my broken foot that was in a cast. I got the injury from walking outside (unrelated to the club). That day, I kept dragging my sore foot around on the floor to avoid being slapped for something I didn't do. Being on the floor gave the appearance that I was trying to solve the problem. You see sometimes I was yelled at and slapped because I didn't solve a problem, or I looked disinterested. On this day, in order to appear helpful, I just kept crawling around so that he would not notice me; I felt like an animal. I felt lower than an animal. Tears were rolling down my face and I was just asking when will all of this be over? And how could this be, God? Where is God in all of this? I wondered, I cried, I prayed. There were times I contemplated suicide, but the thought of leaving my kids behind always kept me wanting to live although I was so miserable. I was so confused. My eyes were swollen and red from crying all the time. My heart would always beat fast if I heard him coming into a room. Sometimes I had panic attacks.

After an intense weekend, on Monday morning, I'd go to work always wondering what just happened. Instead of freaking out, I just kept hearing the words of Pastor Menard in my head, "I'm not abusing you, I'm your father! I can do stuff like this. If you don't like it, get out!" For a few weeks, things would stop, get back to normal, until the next situation. It seemed like the yelling or angry outbursts came in cycles. Pastor Menard was not always hurtful. That's what made things so strange. We had some very good days where things were going well. Parties, fellowships, movies, and heartfelt moments were there at intervals. Sometimes the good times lasted for months, but then something would happen and the slaps, yelling, and fear started all over again.

The men (there were only a few) just seemed to be loyal to him no matter what was happening behind closed doors. I was never sure whether they knew about the sexual relations or not. Eventually they saw the hitting, but they were powerless against what was happening. They assumed kid roles just like the rest of us.

In a nutshell, the pastor could have access to anything he wanted - money, houses, bank accounts, keys to our cars, and any of our personal identification.

Some of us had access to his personal finances too as long as we were respectful to him, to his club, and to his personal family. We trusted each other as long as the pastor was involved.

The club ran the church and some of the members of the church were in the club. For the most part, we acted as a family and Christian business team.

Now looking back on it, sometimes it was like living in a gang because the sole objective became "protecting the pastor." In the beginning the club's philosophy was about helping one another and keeping each other financially, emotionally, and physically strong. As a club, we intended to buy homes, own land, and pursue our dreams together. At least that's what was presented in the beginning.

One of the things that we all had in common as we formed this group was that we all came from some type of broken relationship within our biological families. Having these broken relationships in our biological families seemed to make us cling to each other even more in the club.

As I mentioned before, at first, I enjoyed the club. I believed in the mission and us as a team. The only thing was that in order to continue in the club, I had to give up my own needs, personal desires, and my whole life for someone else to control.

My time no longer belonged to me. Some of the norms of the club played out in the church too. When I worked in the church, my mission was to unselfishly look after the pastor and his needs first, and then the needs of the people in the club. I was a minister for the pastor, not really for God. I was at the pastor's call. We all were. Don't get me wrong, it was a privilege to serve the man of God and we believed (at least I did) that God was pleased with it too. My pastor told us that God was pleased with us if we took care of him, and he often referred to the book of Jeremiah to confirm this. It states, "And God will give you pastors after his own heart…" —Jeremiah 3:15, NLT.

But one day I looked around and noticed that many of us just appeared so sad and depressed, stressed and worn out. One day, I looked out at the club members and observed each of them doing yard work at the pastor's house. Yard work was something that the kids and club members would do together in order to make the pastor's house look its best. It was also time away from church because it would take the place of regular church service. It was something to look forward to for most of us, except for me. Yardwork would start early and last until the evening with a few breaks.

I hated yardwork and I hated to see the staff outside sweating. I didn't like getting dirty and working all day in the hot sun. Sometimes I wondered what the neighbors thought. I guess from the outside looking in, we all looked like slaves. Out in the yard, the children looked tired and were often moody. The club members sometimes looked so exhausted, but to not go the pastor's house for yardwork was interpreted as disrespect. You had better have a very good reason for not participating in making the pastor's house look its best. His own daughters never participated, but the other club kids did. It was a sign of disrespect to refuse. The pastor always seemed offended when club members didn't help. No one wanted to be the person responsible for making the pastor or his family work in the hot sun doing their own yard work.

If you had asked any of the staff whether they hated to work in the pastor's yard, none of them would complain. To some extent, there was something relaxing in doing yard work, but the reality was it was not by choice. It was a convenient way to get favor from the pastor, and that was always a good thing.

The other good thing was that there was usually a pretty good meal for all who participated, and usually the members who did the most work would get paid in play money from the pastor. Don't laugh, this play money was backed by real cash once you cashed it in. The pastor was usually good about paying the team for a job well done.

I sometimes loved the fact the we could miss church in order to do yard work; I just hated being outdoors on these days. I tried to find church office work to do so I could get out of the yard work.

You see, if I had a good excuse for not showing up, then I could be excused and not feel the emotional punishment that could come to me for refusing to "help the pastor with his house."

My point is the club members and the children were not free to say no to yard work which happened mainly during the spring and summer months. Any indication of not wanting to help at the pastor's house ended in an emotional beating from all the club members. As a matter of fact, if you didn't help in bashing the person who refused to help the pastor, then you were also emotionally punished. The pastor would purposely exclude you from the fun gatherings and not allow you to receive new things that others received. This punishment extended to the children and adults. Sometimes children had their names written in the red book for not helping. This was disrespectful to the pastor. Sometimes he was very offended and even angry. The other children were then pressured to shun that child. It was intense, and the guilt and shame that came as a result could make anyone feel two inches tall. The speech usually involved the fact that the pastor gives all of his time to the children in raising them and they can't even come cut grass. On the surface, it really was true that Pastor Menard gave so much to the children and the adults, but the repayment for all his kindness seemed to be never-ending. There was never anything a person could do to satisfy the payment. The repayment for all of his kindness just kept increasing more and more. And as a child, it was overwhelming to have to always want to do yardwork. Sometimes the children wanted to simply be kids and play, but that came with a price. So, most of the kids just went along with the yardwork and found something enjoyable about it when they could.

To put it plainly, most of my life was filled with being strategic about my activities. There was always something the club was doing that we all needed to be a part of every weekend or even every night depending on the urgency. Our lives (including our personal time) belonged to the club, and to have a day off from being or doing what the club wanted required creativity and approval.

My life had become a means to please the club or pastor, and when I wasn't appeasing the club in some form, I had better have a reason why not. There were discussions and meetings that brought peer pressure if you stood out from the norm of the group. In a nutshell, I learned to aim to please.

My whole mission each day was to please the leader, whether I preached a good sermon so that the pastor could have a day off, led a great devotional service in church to comfort the small congregation, conducted a staff meeting enforcing the pastor's wishes, worked on one of our church programs, led a great tear-jerking prayer, handled a difficult caller successfully, or wore a piece of clothing that he liked. I was always careful to ask this one question: "Is this what the pastor wants?"

There were subliminal messages that played in my mind like a tape recorder. "Does my action please the pastor?" Pleasing the pastor was so ingrained into our thinking as a group that the staff would tell it to each other and constantly share our fears of displeasing him.

To understand this better, let's go back to the rank system. If a higher-ranking person in the club said out loud that your actions were not pleasing to the leader, it sent a piercing fear through the whole team. This sting could sometimes last for hours or even days. The feeling that "I'm in trouble" was our constant motivation behind our actions. Many of us lived in this type of fear day in and day out. Fear seemed to be the prevailing feeling whenever we were together. With this constant feeling and voice that said, "You've done something wrong," or "You are in trouble," we were like children trying to find ways to either hide from the pastor or work feverishly to try to please him before he caught us.

I can only speak for myself when I say that I was headed for mental exhaustion. Being a dedicated member of the club, I was driven by a constant fear and need to please our leader. Feeling as if I had done something wrong and having this inward sense all the time that I was never good enough, I served the club and Pastor Menard all I could, trying to prove my loyalty. I did this whether I had done something wrong or not. It was unexplainable.

Even when he wasn't around, like automatons, we policed and regulated one another with words that said, "I'm going to tell on you when the pastor gets here." We would shiver to hear someone say, "I told the pastor what you did." Chills would go through our bodies.

After so much abuse from those words, a few of us found the courage to discuss how we could find better ways to help one another comply with the norms of the club. The funny thing was that discussions about how to please the pastor and stay out of trouble led to us finding friendships with one another. There were times where we were no longer trying to compete against each other for the pastor's approval or attention. Creating these friendships were not easy. This was done very carefully because all friendships were monitored by the leader. And he always found ways to be the go-between with every relationship. We all made it our business to please our leader. When he was happy, the whole team was happy. However, it seemed the more we tried to please him, the more he wanted to be pleased. It was never good enough. The demands from the leader got stronger and more expensive as time went on.

In order to show our devotion, we had to be willing to give our whole paychecks, not just 50% of it. In order to show our devotion, we had to be willing to buy the best Rolex for him despite the cost. In order to show our devotion, we had to be willing to get up in the middle of the night and answer his calls without fail.

Having peace and favor with the leader was the ultimate way to survive. In mastering these two things, a person could live a pretty comfortable life. Accepting the role of a child, we did not question the philosophy of, "do as I say, not as I do ." All staff was supposed to obey this. As long as, I was willing to please the leader, I had favor and was left alone. Things were good for me. But I could never please him enough, and I became exhausted and eventually fell apart. I was mentally unable to keep up with the new demands, moods, and bursts of anger that would come out of nowhere.

Surprisingly, I didn't reach the point of exhaustion until much later in my life. I had lived with the church for nearly 16 years before a big turnaround began.

Many families (outside the club) were leaving the church suddenly without goodbye, without even an explanation. Those of us who remained were always told that the families who left didn't want to be saved and that they were running from the truth; they were not going to be saved long. Our famous phrase was, they can't handle the truth and the pastor's boldness. As a club and church member, I felt blessed because I was able to handle the bold truth that God was giving to us through Pastor Menard.

We who remained felt that we were the true children of God who were strong enough to face the truth of God's word with the direct boldness of an anointed man of God, our pastor.

Despite that confidence, I had another feeling raging inside me too. All along I felt like my life was slowly being destroyed. I didn't fight because I didn't think I had to. Somehow, I thought that my life was what it was supposed to be. I didn't suspect anything. I didn't say a mumbling word, so the destruction just continued.

The person that I wanted to be was being destroyed by my obligation to serve the club, and ultimately, the pastor. Don't get me wrong. I wanted to serve the Pastor; I just didn't want to give up my true identity in order to do it. There were times where I wasn't sure whether I was serving God, the pastor, or something else. If serving the pastor meant abandoning God, then that was not what I signed up for.

Everything I said, felt, or saw was what the pastor or group wanted. In reality, it seemed that I had lost touch with what I wanted. I knew that my personal feelings were irrelevant if they were not in agreement with the pastor's desire for me. To me, I was sacrificing and denying myself for the work of the ministry. However, it was extremely difficult for me to tell whether our club was really following the holy Scriptures. The sacrificing didn't feel right anymore. And the bottom line seemed to be that all we had to do was follow the pastor's word (whether he was following the Scriptures or not).

Chapter 5
This is Killing Me

Call Him Daddy

Since the beginning of this writing, I told you about my life, but what about my kids? I realize now just how much my decisions affected my children. For several years, I worked in the church before taking an outside job. During the years that I worked for the church, I decided to homeschool my children. I was inspired to do this when I realized that the public -school system failed them. My kids were slowly showing signs of rebellion, and school officials appeared to be labelling my sons as problem students. My daughter was simply neglected by the school system. Because she was never a behavior problem, she was passed to the next grades without actually knowing the work. I had to do something. There was so much that went into this decision and so many adjustments that had to be made that it would take another book to explain it. What is clear is that the very act of homeschooling my children is probably what saved their lives when everything in the church took a turn for the worst. In hindsight, this intervention prepared them and me for the one of the greatest trials of our lives.

You see, my children were the first students in the church to be homeschooled. I was their teacher, and since I worked at the church, I taught them at the church every day before I went to school at night. I was homeschooling while attending graduate school at night to complete my master's degree.

My children were pre-teens at the time. As anyone could imagine, they were not happy having their mom as their teacher. We were together every day, almost all day. Teens want their freedom from their mom. I understood that back then, but I was sure that homeschooling them was what God wanted me to do. So, I did it relentlessly.

Before long, some of the other children from the club members' families joined the homeschool, and later this group became the Christian school. There were approximately 10 to 12 students in the school, all at different ages. They all belonged to our church and were members of the club because of their parents.

Naturally, the Christian school enjoyed the privileges of having parents who belonged to the club. We lived hastle-free when it came to having resources and a support group. The Christian school operated in the church, and it became the church's K-12 school. The Christian school was just another privilege to the parents who were in the club because a few of their children were having trouble in school too. I was head of the school and never wanted the club to control it because the inspiration came to me. No one else wanted to do it, and I had a passion for it. However, I lost that battle. Ultimately, Pastor Menard was the figure head for the school while I ran it. I did all the work and I enjoyed that part of it. He, however, took the credit.

Nonetheless, the Christian school was my baby, so to speak, but it was still controlled by the club. The club controlled everything and everybody and the pastor was the leader of the club and church.

The school operated every day at the church. Our school was registered with the state and was a member of a larger organization. There were formal training, curriculum and regulatory guidelines that we met in order to operate. All the children were attending classes, completing assignments, research and homework. Sometimes the work required hours and hours of study. Not only were children in classes, but they were learning leadership, organizational and job skills by doing volunteer work at the church helping with the various ministries. Some days were very long for me and the kids. Because the school was monitored by Pastor Menard, there was no such thing as missing assignments or misbehaving in class. He was informed of everything and was a part of almost everything that the school did. Any form of disrespect toward parents or volunteer teachers was met with swift and certain punishment from the pastor, which brings me to one of the most difficult parts of my testimony…the life that my children had to endure. The school existed for approximately two years before things changed.

When do you know that you have had enough of something? I mean, really, what does it take?

As humans we all experience pain, but some of us can continue doing the same hurtful things over and over again because it fulfills something inside. It doesn't matter that it may be killing us. As humans, we can keep overeating, smoking, spending, gossiping, or hating because it makes us feel a certain way.

You see, it felt good to Pastor Menard to receive power, attention, and respect, even when it came from a place of fear. I didn't know it then, but now I see that he continued to create situations of dependency, control, and pain. Whenever those three things were present, he seemed to be his best. I had the tendency to "put out the fires." I knew how to smooth things over and fix problems even when it came from a place of fear. Where there was fear, pain and discomfort, I ran to the rescue, but never really looked at the impact of the damage that was being done. I guess you could say that I got gratification in some way from rescuing everybody. I just didn't realize how dysfunctional this was. I'll explain this a little further.

Whether they were in Christian school, public school, or homeschool, the children were expected to do their assignments and chores at home. And the pastor had very strict rules for all the kids.

After being away running errands, there were times when I would walk into the church and hear the cries of the children who just got in trouble for bad grades. At first, it sounded normal to me - they deserved the spanking because they got bad grades, right? They didn't take out the trash. They didn't turn in their report cards. They disrespected the teacher at school. They didn't do their chores. They were spanked for any appearance of bad behavior. We parents stood by while the pastor spanked the children. We believed that to interfere with the discipline of your child was to poison your child and deny the pastor the right to exercise "fatherly" control.

I understood this at first. I was convinced that as a single parent I needed the guidance, experience, and correction of my fatherly pastor. In my mind and heart, I was not wrong. I was right. I wanted my children to be leaders and I knew that would take a strong hand since I was raising them without a father.

In the beginning, my pastor was doing a good job of helping me and the other moms, but there was always a sense of when is it enough? I wondered if it was necessary for him to always do the disciplining. I mean, we as mothers were capable sometimes, right? He didn't think so. As a matter of fact, all the women seemed to doubt their own parenting skills and willingly chose to allow the pastor to discipline her children.

However, deep inside I wondered whether he enjoyed disciplining the children because he seemed to have a look on his face of disgust and satisfaction at the same time. The room would be filled with kids crying while their mothers were sad and trying to explain the reasons for their kids' behaviors. I can remember long speeches and agonizing questioning that the kids endured. The kids lied to keep from getting punishment, and for this there would be more punishment. However, I noticed that there were times when the kids were not lying, but their expressions didn't meet the pastor's approval. He would become angry, and they still got in trouble. It was terrorizing to be in these meetings because of the emotional exhaustion it brought to everyone involved. Sometimes it was a huge dramatic scene. I just couldn't understand though why Pastor Menard had this peculiar look on his face at times.

When will I be good enough to handle my own kids without the pastor's help? That day never came. I was never good enough. Any decision I made in disciplining them always seemed wrong. The pastor would scold me for making parental decisions that he did not agree with. Fearing to make the wrong decisions, I would always confer with Pastor Menard first. This was a way of life for me and my kids, and the other mothers did the same. Pastor Menard was not just a pastor; he was a father to me and to my kids, but he also seemed to be becoming something else too.

I didn't always agree with his decisions. Some of his ways of discipline seemed excessive. When I told him about my concerns, he would adjust his methods temporarily; however, he always seemed offended that I would question him at these moments.

Sometimes I was the topic of the meeting to the rest of the mothers when I exercised my right to speak up. It was perceived that I did not trust him, so my kids were shunned whenever I spoke up on their behalf. As a mother, I felt so bad. After speaking against his method of discipline, I would watch the other kids ignore my children. The pastor would do nice things for the other children (excluding my kids) because I expressed doubt about his methods. The children didn't understand the emotional shunning they were receiving; sometimes even the adults would shun my kids if they knew that Pastor Menard was offended by something I said. To see this happening made me feel like I had done something wrong. And then I felt like an even worse mom than before. This cycle continued.

Just like being in the club, Pastor Menard would constantly say, "You can get out of the club," and "If you don't want me to discipline your kids, then just say so and I'll leave you and your kids alone." The other part to that was they would no longer be able to sing in the choir, play with his children, or get the attention that the other kids got. They would be outcasts. We were with the church everyday including weekends, and it was humiliating to see my children the object of ridicule and rejection for weeks.

Overall, my children lived as outcasts more than the other kids, for many reasons. The number one reason was because I expressed my concerns to Pastor Menard regarding his methods of discipline. Doing this caused tension and what appeared to be retaliation. Back then I didn't know what it was called. All I knew was that my kids and I were feeling like criminals at these moments. The feeling was strong and lingered for several days or weeks. It was terrible. As you guessed it, I learned to back down. After a while, I became silent because I also was emotionally punished by the other adults for speaking my mind. Everyone thought that I was not grateful for Pastor Menard's help. I would receive speeches from club members about how this behavior was showing unfaithfulness. I backed down unless there was something that I just couldn't handle seeing. I agreed to have Pastor Menard discipline my children because I really believed that it was God's will for him to be in their lives. I didn't want to interfere with God's will for my children, so I grinned and bore the discipline they received. Any time I was present, I never saw him intentionally, physically abuse any of the children in the church.

Pastor Menard never left physical marks on my kids; he never caused any broken bones, and I don't believe he ever intentionally tried to hurt them. If I ever suspected these things to be true, I would have run from this church as fast as I could no matter how much it would have cost. I never saw bruises on my children nor scars. What I did see was fear in their eyes each time he spanked them. He never spanked them without them understanding what the spanking was about. He spent a long and tedious time explaining why he was giving them the punishment, whether it was a spanking, or extra chores, or the like.

He was so obsessive about any small behavior that it seemed they were punished for every little thing. He seemed to be irritated a lot. They were punished excessively too. For example, if they missed the bus to school, they would have to pay unreasonable amounts of money (that kids their age would normally not have) for the misconduct. If they didn't have the money, they would have to earn it by doing chores at the church, at home, or at someone else's home. The chores included doing yard work, cleaning the garage, or being the dishwasher for months. I guess I could live with those types of punishments. It's the other things that often made me cry as a mother. Sometimes he would have them spend days living in the garage in order to teach them to appreciate cleanliness. These methods seemed too excessive at times, but I never saw that they harmed my kids in any way. At that time, the most they endured was embarrassment, or so I thought.

Watching my children endure this was very hard on me at times. Thankfully, there were times that Pastor Menard listened to my suggestions in finding other ways to handle discipline.

As the children got older, the above methods seemed unnecessary, and other ways of discipline were used for a while.

For example, if a child was being disrespectful at home with a parent, the other club members would allow the child being disciplined to move in for weeks with them so that the child could experience "time out" away from his mother. Although I trusted the other club members, I didn't like that I could not see my kids for days when they were away. However, we, as a family, got through it.

The idea behind sending them to each other's homes was tough love. I believed that the "time out" was a deterrent from jail later as adults. I, like the others, trusted that this was necessary in keeping our children from becoming delinquent. Pastor Menard explained how our children were headed for juvenile delinquency unless there was intervention. His discipline was intervention, and it was emotionally draining for my children as well as for me. I didn't know how to raise children, especially boys, and I trusted Pastor Menard even when my heart was so heavy, I could hardly keep it together inside.

What I knew was that I prayed, prayed, prayed, prayed, and cried, and prayed for my kids as I witnessed what appeared to be very grueling discipline. Was it psychological abuse and emotional abuse? Back then, I could not tell. I had no words to describe how everything felt.

I tried to rationalize it. I tried to minimize the horror of seeing my children placed in "jail" for bad behavior. But I, as a club member, allowed my children to be disciplined this way in hopes that it was making them into better kids.

The pretend "jail" was a space or room in the house that acted as the punishment place. Sometimes that place was in the bathroom, kitchen, or at another's house. The child who was being punished had to sit in this space for hours, sometimes days.

They were always fed, but they sometimes had little contact with their mother. As parents we wanted to see our children, but to do that would mean that we would suffer some type of emotional or psychological punishment too. One punishment that often happened was that our children would have to stay longer on the punishment if we (as the parent) interfered with the punishment. No mother wanted that to happen, so we endured the punishment emotionally while our child was in "jail." While at another club member's house, we trusted each other, so we never worried about whether our children were safe. I was not worried about that.

Because we were all family, we knew that our children were okay. The main concern was about the mother who wanted to speak against this method but was forced to remain silent through peer-pressure. If parents disagreed with the radical methods the pastor used to discipline the children, they were ridiculed and labelled as unfaithful to the club and accused of refusing help from the man of God. The children of that parent were also pressured to shun their own parents who tried to protect them. The child would feel that they got their parent in trouble based on their own behavior that caused the spanking in the first place. It was quite complicated. The children regulated their parents and the parents regulated their children while Pastor Menard remained in the middle of the parent-child relationship.

In some cases, it seemed that the parent was pitted against her own child if she tried to interfere with the discipline. She was made to feel that she was hurting her child more by not allowing the pastor to help "save" the child.

The discipline could be summed up like this. The child and parent were both disciplined by Pastor Menard, and many times, in front of one another. The philosophy was that he had to spank your child. You had to spank your child. He had to slap your face in front of your child so that you and your child understood that you both were subject to him as the father of the family. I guess you could say he was establishing authority, and it worked. We all respected Pastor Menard and felt he had our best interest at heart.

This is what fathers do, right? We were all his children and he made it clear that nobody, absolutely nobody would disrespect his authority! The physical spankings were just enough so that no harm was done. What I didn't realize then was that the effects of the spankings continued long after the physical pain. I learned later that my children continued to spank themselves psychologically by always being fearful of making mistakes and being reluctant to share their true feelings. To my surprise, the discipline seemed to be having more of a negative effect. Rather than love and admiration for the tough love they received, my children seemed to be developing resentment.

They were fearful to share their failures or opinions. They were fearful of confiding in us, their parents, who had to report their behaviors to the pastor; the same was true for the children. They were obligated to report their parents' behavior to the pastor. The dynamic became parent against child, child against parent. I always hated this, but I kept thinking that I would be displeasing God if I ever disagreed with this type of arrangement. There were times where I was afraid to say things around my children at home because of fear that it would get back to Pastor Menard. I've been in many situations where I was actually defending my actions to the pastor for something I said to my children in my own home. It seemed like there were no boundaries. Our relationship was constantly regulated by the pastor.

Any sign of disrespect toward the pastor that happened in our private homes had to be reported to the pastor. The pastor would ask mothers to tell on their kids. He would have children to tell on their parents and on their siblings. Whoever was the snitch was rewarded. As a result, I suppose the children learned to distrust their parents and vice versa. They learned that their parents had no real authority. Their parents were, in a lot of cases, one of them, a child. The point is that if the child had feelings that they wanted to share with their parents alone, they could not. The parent was obligated to share what their kids told them. This created a reluctance to share their feelings with the parents directly. Parents also would not share their thoughts against the pastor to their kids. All communication seemed to go through Pastor Menard.

As a mother, I would hide my sympathy for my children. I would only show my disgust towards them for their behavior, but seldom would I show them my love. Showing sympathy or love to my kids was considered being weak, and Pastor Menard seemed to hate weakness.

By carefully choosing my words, I learned to mask my disagreement of the pastor from my kids so that neither of us would be forced to tell on each other. I believe that neither the mothers nor their children wanted to see one another be scolded or punished.

My concern was that our children were punished for things that were not always bad behavior. Not all of the behaviors were bad, but if the pastor thought it was bad, then it was bad. The problem was that ANY defiant behavior was met with punishments that didn't always fit the crime. For example, if my child got a bad grade in school, he would be spanked in front of the other children in the club, or he would have to pay an astronomical fine, do extra chores and get his name written in what we called the "red book." Each of the children experienced this, but it seemed that my children experienced this the most.

I felt like this was very excessive, and they would be on punishment for weeks and sometimes months. I never understood why my children seemed to receive greater punishments as they got older. Maybe it was because they had a tendency to ask the wrong questions to the pastor while trying to reason with him at the wrong times.

Nonetheless, my children were punished the most. The pastor did not like being questioned, especially when it came to his disciplinary actions. Now let's talk about the "red book." This was a book that was originally designed to give the club kids recognition for any good behaviors. Like most things, it began as something good, and it was started by the pastor pertaining only to the club families. As a child, having your name written in this book meant you could enjoy extra privileges and obtain money for any outstanding achievements. The kids were honored for being "Youth of the Month" at church or for honor roll achievement from public school. It started as a good idea; along the way, the book's intent began to change into the "book of all behaviors," not just good behaviors. As the focus of it got lost, it later served as a punishment book for all the kids who did bad things. The book held their names and their offenses. There was a person who was usually in charge of making sure the punishments were carried out based on what was written in the book.

Just like the club's mission changed, the book's purpose changed too. It later served as a method to control the behavior of the children. The "red book" was used as punishment along with the spankings.

None of the children wanted their names to be written in the red book. Even we as the parents were often fearful that our kids' names would be in the book for infractions. Sometimes their punishments would be weeks of hard labor (chores around the church or at one of the club member's homes). As a parent, I felt sorry for the children who had their names in the book. And once again, my sons had their names in the book most of the time. It seemed they were always in trouble, and no matter how much they tried to do the right things and say the right things, they were never good enough in the sight of the pastor. I remember trying to talk to Pastor Menard about why he was so mean to my kids. He would never say why; there was never a reason. My kids were just considered the most troublesome of the kids. I believed this lie for a long time until one day I woke up. Unfortunately, it was a little too late. Keep reading, I'll explain why.

Having a book of punishments and rules of behavior for the kids was the same as having rules and disciplinary actions for the adults in the club. Everything started looking the same. The club had rules too.

Before long, it seemed there were no real distinctions between me and my children in the eyes of the pastor. He punished both child and parent if they got out of line. A mother was slapped or made to do extra chores if she was not reverent enough. This type of control was not just evident between the pastor and the mother. If one mother was not reverent enough to the pastor, the other mothers would view her in disgust, shame, and she was shunned. Her own child was expected to shun his mother if his mom was on the pastor's bad list for the month.

Notice that I am referring to the mothers mainly. That's because we mainly had single moms in our church. There were only a couple of fathers who were present, and they were never slapped. If they were disrespectful to the pastor, they were just berated verbally by the pastor in front of their wives. The pastor tried to maintain emotional control of the wives in the marriages that were there. Many marriages did not survive long under these conditions.

Trying to be supportive of the pastor's style, I tried to make sense of things, but was often confused about why the punishments seemed so long, so punitive, so constant, and so intense. I never had a father in my home while I was growing up. Is this the way it was supposed to be? In frustration and stress, I cried out to God many, many nights, saying, "Why is this happening to me?"

My prayer to God...

I can't do this alone. Why did my father ever leave me when I was a child? If he was in my life, then I wouldn't need Pastor Menard. Why did my grandfather have to die when I was young? He was the only father figure I knew. Why do I need the pastor in my life like this? Where is my kids' father? Why did we have to break up? Where is the help, God? Please send some help! He seems like he is so angry, he's so rough, he's so mean, but I can't raise these kids on my own...I'm all alone!! I'm glad I never had to be raised by Pastor Menard. I would hate being a kid if he were my real father!

Even in these prayers, I still held on to the idea that Pastor Menard was supposed to be a father to my kids. I kept believing it was the will of God. This break down would come in cycles in my head year after year. I would pray the same prayer over and over to God regarding the discipline of my kids. Then the crying would stop and somehow, I knew this was my life. I was being raised by pastor Menard and I hated it. I began to hate it more and more each day.

It never occurred to me that maybe God never told Pastor Menard to raise my kids, or maybe God never intended for me to be with this church. Each time, though, I would revert back to the same thought, which was although I hated it, it was God's will for me to be here (at least that's what I thought).

Over and over in my mind I wondered when it was enough. How could the pastor see mothers and daughters on the same level as each other, and sons and their fathers on the same level too? How is it that Pastor Menard saw the club members as kids? We are not kids! But God why won't you tell him? He can't see us! Why can't he see that we are not kids?

Journal Entry

Will the pastor stop spanking my children now that they are screaming? Will the pastor stop spanking my kids now that all the other children are standing around in terror? Will the pastor stop spanking my kids now that their backs were hurting?

Will he stop slapping me while my son looks on? Will he stop yelling at me as my children hang down their heads? Will he stop being offended when I try to tell him to leave my children alone because they are shaking, standing there ashamed? Why does the pastor encourage the other kids to shame my kids? Doesn't he see members standing in silence wanting to help my child who is publicly humiliated and ridiculed? When is it enough?

Psychologically, as a family, my kids and I continued to regulate each other's behaviors, and we reported those behaviors to the pastor, even when there were times that I just wanted to handle my own children's lives. All I wanted was for my kids to see Pastor Menard as their father figure, not their punisher. That never happened. It seemed that my children and I became divided and distrusting of each other. I didn't know them, and they didn't know me.
Enough is enough!

I Had to Stay!

Each year, the turmoil of understanding why I felt so trapped continued to plague me. I thought within myself, "I'm saved and I'm doing God's will, so why do I feel so stressed, so fearful, so confused?"

I believed that I was being unfaithful by having (silent) alternate points of view from the pastor. I believed that I was displeasing God by doubting the actions of my pastor, the man of God. Each time I had doubt or disagreement, I kept it inside and prayed that it would go away. I was always fearful of being the Judas in the group. Judas betrayed Jesus Christ. Was I going to be the one who betrayed the pastor? The pastor often talked about all the people who abandoned his ministry and how much he was let down by those people. I never wanted to be "those people" who left the pastor when all he was trying to do was help their families.

Although I disagreed with some of the disciplinary methods, I was conditioned to believe that the spankings and punishment were necessary for my children's success. Besides, I was raising two boys who were already targets in our society. I knew that as African American boys, our society already viewed them as criminals. Black boys were known for going to juvenile court. It was like the norm or somethin'. By allowing the pastor to father them, I thought I was I preventing them from going to jail. I prayed that all my children be focused, hard workers, responsible for their own behaviors, and respectful to authority. My sons desired to be successful, and I as their mother was going to make it happen, even if it made me cry.

I felt I was protecting my daughter from being a teenage mom by having her to be disciplined by the pastor. I did not want her to live her life forever on food stamps. I was determined to save my children, even if it meant physical punishment for me or them. Being spanked when I was a child was never a crime. When I was young, my mother spanked my sister and me. Thankfully, she stopped when we learned the lessons. She never abused us as kids, and I always knew she loved us. I believe spanking should be done in love and only as the last resort.

While my children were young, I figured that having it tough while they were young meant they would not make unnecessary mistakes when they got older.

African American boys are targets of relentless discrimination and abuse in our society today. I believe there are still people, institutions. and policies or laws designed to either bring down the black male or incarcerate him. I didn't want my sons to be victims, and I was afraid for their lives ALL THE TIME!

If my daughter didn't learn anything else, I was going to make sure she would learn to be self-sufficient, never having to lean on anyone for her self-worth. So yes, I went along with what we call "tough love." Please forgive me if I was too timid to recognize the difference between love and hate. Did my pastor love my children and was that the reason he seemed to always find time to spank them? Or did my pastor hate my children because they were the offspring of my husband and that's the reason he always spanked them over what seemed to be small matters? At that time, I could not tell.

As I stated earlier, they were sometimes punished for things that were not so much bad behaviors, just bad decisions that could have been corrected with a lecture. Lectures were used at times and that would be the extent of the punishment, but whenever the pastor was in a bad mood, things were worse.

Punishments were so punitive that sometimes the kids were punished for having bad thoughts. If the pastor thought the kids were thinking things against him, he would punish the kids. He would say, "I know what you're thinking," and then he would punish them. To disagree with him would mean more punishment. I prayed, prayed, and prayed for my kids, but I grew more and more afraid of the pastor each day. He kept telling me it was God's will for him to be the way he was with my children. There were many nights I cried trying to understand why God was so hard on my kids through the pastor. Why my kids?

Only by God's mercy were my children able to withstand the punishments every year as they got older.

As stated earlier, as a parent, I was emotionally and psychologically pressured and shamed whenever I tried to intervene with the pastor's discipline. Sometimes my intervention would cause the punishments to be worse for the kids, especially for my sons. Over time, I learned how to soothe the pastor so that he would be nicer to my kids.

In retrospect, I can see that maybe God was answering my prayers after all. I had to attend a mandatory domestic violence seminar for my job. This was a subject that I didn't think I needed. I never thought I was in a domestic violence situation. Who ever heard of domestic violence between pastor and his staff? That's stupid and unheard of. It was hard to believe I was in an abusive environment.

Plenty of times, Pastor Menard assured all of us that if he were an abuser, he would not be able to control the force of his slaps. He assured us that the type of physical contact he had with us was never damaging and he could stop at any time. Furthermore, he said that he didn't intend to stop because he was not doing anything wrong. I understood this and believed it for a long time, however, after attending the seminar on domestic violence, I saw many similarities. I slowly began to wonder how what he was doing was any different. It was just a thought that I kept dismissing.

In the seminar I learned that with the cycle of domestic abuse, there were times where things were okay. Oh my God! That was what I saw with the club family. There were good times where the club kids enjoyed a normal life. The individual families would participate in family time, parents would discipline their own children for a while, and the kids could enjoy regular activities (i.e. going to movies, having parties, playing games/sports, etc...) without the threat of the pastor in our affairs. He was nice and seemed to support all the families. The problem was we never knew when the next round of harsh disciplinary actions would come again. As my children got older, the pastor got more unpredictable in his discipline toward them. The punishments were for very small things, and the children (like the club members) were becoming exhausted in trying to please the pastor before he had another outburst of anger. Although I could tell that the relationship between him and the children was becoming resentful because the kids stopped showing signs of any emotions, there were times when I thought my kids and Pastor Menard had some type of special relationship. Many times, I was jealous of their relationship.

You see, he would tell me that my kids confided in him and that they didn't trust me as their mom. He would say that he understood them and that I didn't. It reminded me of what happened with my husband and me some years ago. Pastor Menard used to tell me that my husband confided in him and that I could not ask my husband any questions about what the pastor shared with me about his confessions. Again, it seemed the pastor was the center of my relationship with my family - first my husband and now my kids.

Pastor Menard told me that he heard the confessions from my kids, and he was the only one who could help them with their issues. Pastor Menard shared a few of their confessions with me, and he promised he was going to help them. In order for my kids to continue to confide in him and receive help, I was not to tell my kids that I knew the confessions that they shared with the pastor. Boy! As I reflected on this years later, it hit me. It sounded too familiar. This was the same thing Pastor Menard told me about my ex-husband! I was led to believe that without the pastor's guidance in my family, my relationship with my kids would be destroyed. For fear of losing my kids, I included pastor Menard in practically every decision regarding my children. Consequently, the trust and relationship between my kids and me was almost non- existent, but I still didn't see the impact it was having on all of us.

This relationship where Pastor Menard was the mediator between my kids and me lasted for a number of years. After a while there was very little that we discussed without the pastor knowing. It became normal, although exhausting.

However, things began to shift. Most of the club children were becoming teens who, after a while, were not willing to take the punishments any longer. They appeared emotionless, numb, and seemed to deal with the punishments with callousness. I didn't know then, but later I learned that my children and the other club kids learned how to soothe the pastor just like the mothers were doing. The only difference was that they were bold enough to talk behind his back. In public, they showed honor and respect to him, but behind closed doors all the kids learned to keep their real feelings from their parents and from him. Some of the children formed bonds and secrets among themselves. Somehow, they became their own family without including us as their parents. Being the Christian school administrator, I felt like I still had a rapport with them. They didn't tell me everything, but I felt like they would share the most important things with me.

To be honest, there was a part of me that felt relieved (in some sense) because it seemed that the kids had an outlet among each other. I never let on that I approved of their kid family group, and to the best of my ability I would protect their group by becoming a supporter of their teamwork. I was still holding on to the belief that all the punishments were for their own good, but I also liked the idea that they were able to find strength in each other when the pressure was too much.

I understood the pressure they had to endure as teens, although I did not agree with them being disrespectful to authority as a means of dealing with their frustration. In other words, I supported them as long as they did their best in obeying the rules. For instance, they needed to do their homework, not date without parental approval, and respect authority. Those were just a few.

I thought that having bonds with each other was a healthy way of dealing with teen life. In essence, I protected their teen family by expressing to the club members and pastor how positive it was that they were learning teamwork.

Using my influence as the administrator of our Christian school, I told Pastor Menard that it was good to encourage some type of community among the youth. He agreed.

I would encourage them to work together on projects, school assignments, and plan social outings that they enjoyed. I publicly supported them by presenting this in a positive light to the pastor. The funny thing was that I really did support this teamwork and really did think it was a positive thing for them until everything took a turn for the worst (or at least that's what I thought). Read a little further to see how this played out.

Meanwhile, I hated to see my children spanked, and I started harboring some doubt, distrust toward the pastor. Out of all the parents, it seemed that I could talk to him more. In some sense, I was like the head mother when it came to the relationship between the pastor and the club mothers. But even with the little influence I had, it seemed that he would continue with his own beliefs. At times however, he would see my point of view, promise to make changes, but without fail, he would then revert back to his original methods in just a short while.

Having seen this pattern many times, I learned to soothe the pastor, not because I trusted him as a father, but because I loved my children and didn't want to see him punish them. I would find ways to show him the good in all the children. Somehow, I felt it was my duty to "protect them" from him. I played the role as "mother for all the children."

Whenever I could, I stood up for them and prayed for them all. I prayed for the protection of my children. I prayed for the protection of the club members in the church. I prayed for myself that I could continue in the church where I believed God had placed me.

Then the weirdest thing happened. The children were becoming less fearful of the pastor. I couldn't believe my eyes. I thought they were losing their minds. They were not verbally disrespectful, but they were more relaxed in their approach to him and they appeared to laugh things off whenever they were in trouble. I also saw them console each other and take punishments for one other. It was like a brotherhood of some type that was developing among the kids. They were protecting each other!

The more I prayed and cried out to Jesus for them, it seemed that my perception was slowly changing to something that I could not put my finger on. I didn't feel the same, and it was very uncomfortable. Later, I learned that from interceding in prayer for the kids and their parents that something was not quite right in the club, but I still could not put my finger on it. Was God hearing me? Was I hearing God?

But rather than seeing change, I noticed that the pastor became more aggressive with some of the mothers. Instead of just slapping them, he now was grabbing and shaking them more. I would come into the church during the day after having been at my college classes to find that some of the mothers had swollen and red eyes. I knew this meant that they had been hit by or had gotten in trouble with the pastor. The norm was not to ask questions and just assume that naturally it was the mother's fault. It was always the women's fault for why the pastor would lash out. Things would be very quiet, and everyone knew to be even nicer to the pastor or your turn could be next.

Let me say here for those of you who are saying, "How could you be so blind? This man was abusing you all!" Just hear me out. It was very hard to accuse Pastor Menard of abuse. None of us had any lasting scars. We still could function at our jobs and schools. None of us were malnourished or lacked any physical need. How could we say we were abused? Remember, we had adopted the idea that we were his spiritual children (not his equal). Most of us had adopted this when we were literally 18 or 19 years old. Most of us had just left our biological parent's home, or abusive relationships, and entered into this new way of living. It felt like adulthood with training wheels so to speak.

This is a very powerful concept that many who are outside of abusive relationships do not understand. The reason why so much abuse is tolerated in families, marriages, organizations, and even churches, is the idea that the abused is in fact inferior. The abused person has to accept inferiority as a reality in order for the abuser to have his power. I remember a quote from someone who said that being inferior is a choice. However, I'm not sure that is true for every situation.

The truth is, I chose to be subservient to our pastor because I trusted, revered, and honored him on the level of God's representative. Secondly, I came from other dysfunctional and abusive relationships where boundaries were blurred. Living like this was a step up from those other relationships that I experienced. Third, I was looking for acceptance, belonging, and a father figure. Pastor Menard provided the missing pieces in my life. He also encouraged me to go back to school, get my degree, and become a better person. Many of us there had that testimony. Therefore, to suddenly believe that he was a criminal was unthinkable and hard to accept. I had to stay to support him and the church.

Something went wrong, very wrong!

While my testimony of becoming better in my life was true, there was still something very wrong. I began to notice that the more I prayed, the more I saw there was a difference between what the God of the Bible looked like and what the god of my pastor looked like. Was I serving the wrong god? Or was my pastor serving the wrong god? All I knew was that my prayers were not working!

Suddenly something was happening that was much greater than I was. Something was happening around me, but I just didn't know what it was. The most I can tell you is that I began to see and believe that spiritually the pastor was my god! I didn't want the pastor to be my god, but that's who he seemed to be, and in a big way! Although feeling this way, I still did not fully consider this until 2002, two years after the Christian school was established.

One day the pastor, the club staff, and I were doing some spring cleaning at our storage facility. On that day, my pastor received a phone call from his wife. He spoke to her briefly before he slowly walked into the room where I was working on my final take home exam from college.

I was working on my paper while the other club members were working in the shed. He had a worried look on his face as he nervously said to me, "I got to go home. My wife just called and said that one of the girls from the church accused me of rape." He left immediately.

You see, the night prior to this, the club kids went out for ice cream. The pastor's older daughter, who was about 19 years old, had taken some of the kids out for the ice cream when one of the children began to disclose to the pastor's daughter that she had been sexually molested.

The girl was sister Tasha's daughter. Of all the club kids, there were approximately seven children, and four of them were between the ages of 14 to 17 years old. It's important to point out now that when I refer to the club kids, I am not referring to the pastor's own kids. He had two girls, but they were never a part of the club kids. For the most part, the pastor's kids and his wife remained neutral parties when it came to the affairs of the club or the church. We, as club members, only visited them from time to time at their house, and they came to church and went home. To my knowledge, they were never aware of the club norms except what was shared with them by the pastor. For some reason, he never liked any of us sharing any information about the club with his personal family. He made us feel like it was privileged information; even his wife and children were not allowed to know our club affairs.

Anyway, on this night the pastor said to me that one of the kids just accused him of rape. As he was packing to leave the house like a flash, I was frozen with fear. I gathered my things, as did the rest of the staff, and we all headed to our individual homes. Although one child was named, we got wind that all the club children were involved in what appeared to be a scandal.

When I entered my home, my children were already there. My three children were approximately 14 to 15 years old at the time. I remember that as I walked through the door that night, they were ranting and raving about how our lives had been a lie. The lie was that we were not this Christian family (as it was presented to them), the pastor was not their spiritual father and we as a church were not following the word of God. In their minds everything was a lie.

My son, who never raised his voice to me in the past, now began accusing me and saying that I, somehow, knew what he was talking about. I did not know what he was talking about!

I said to him, with alarm in my voice, "What's wrong with you?" I don't know what you're talking about." He yelled back, "Don't act like you don't know!" I was at a loss for words. He further stated, "All of you are having sex with the pastor. Don't act like you don't know." I stood there in shock.

My other two children began telling me that they (all the teen children) were at the ice cream restaurant and a girl from the group began telling everyone that she had been molested by the pastor.

My children began speaking about how they were being mistreated by the pastor and the conversation between us just escalated. There were no words I could use to console them. They were convinced that I and the other adult church/club members were liars.

The details of the conversation they had at the ice cream shop were never revealed to me. All I knew was that the pastor's daughter taped the whole session on a cassette- tape and she gave it to the pastor's wife (her mother).

After receiving the cassette, Sis. Menard immediately called the pastor (her husband), and he denied ever doing this with this young girl who was about 16 years old at the time.

The pastor's daughter ended up sharing this recording with a former member of the church who was not a club member. Apparently, according to this former member, the things that were recorded about the pastor were so horrific that the pastor's daughter was advised to contact the police, and she did.

After the police were notified, a full investigation was launched against the pastor and our church. There were allegations that he had sexually molested this young girl who was the daughter of one of the club members.

I don't need to tell you that literally everything in our lives stopped. By the following week, the girl who made the allegations, along with her teenage brother, were removed from their homes by the Department of Children Services.

My children were still in my custody, but I was called in by police for questioning with detectives and social workers.

Quickly, the investigation became one about the whole church, not just the pastor. It was during this investigation that I learned the pastor had already been accused of another rape in California. It was not clear whether this was the real reason why several years ago we packed up and moved from that state. Up to this point in the investigation, I had never known that he had formerly been accused of rape.

With intense fear surrounding me, I had a choice to make. I was either going to believe his innocence and stick with my pastor of whom I had known for nearly 20 years, or believe the story of this one child and the group of law enforcers trying to make a name for themselves through intimidation and exaggeration.

At first, it was not a hard decision for me. I believed that my pastor would never do such a thing and the girl who made the allegations was not believable. I knew her fairly well. She had some problems with being kicked out of public school, telling lies, arranging meetings with men and other boys she met on the internet, and consistently disrespecting her mom. Her mom and I worked together to get her some help when she was failing school. There were some slight improvements in her life although she was struggling in a lot of areas.

Although struggling in her self- esteem, she was not a bad child. I was proud of the gains we made in getting her the academic help she needed and was pretty confident that she would try to inform me if anything had ever happened to her.

I thought that she looked up to me as her mentor, and we appeared to have a good relationship at that time. That's why it was so difficult to understand why she never told me anything. There were no visible signs of any sexual abuse. I believed that she and I had a good enough relationship that she could have shared this with me. She never shared anything like this with me.

Nonetheless, when the allegations were made, she and I never spoke again. We were not allowed to speak to each other based on the investigation. Our church was literally torn apart. There were no supporters in the community that came to our rescue. It seemed that news reporters, radio media, neighbors, law enforcement, and even family members did not want to have anything to do with us or our church. As far as the outside world was concerned, our pastor was guilty until proven innocent.

My life changed forever from this event. Within the following weeks, my children were removed, and eventually the children from all the club families were taken away, one family at a time, and placed in state custody. Unexpectedly, I guess my chance at being somebody had finally come true. My whole life was exposed in front of hundreds of people because it hit the newspapers. My pastor had several charges of child rape against him, and after some time, some of those allegations eventually came from my own daughter.

I went to court to plead to the judge that I was a good mother, but the judge had rubber stamped the petition papers. Off my children went into state custody for what seemed the rest of their teenage lives until my mother-in-law took them in.

You see, after my children were taken from me on the premise that the church was a sexually abusive environment, I was informed that my daughter started making allegations against the pastor too. Another club member's child made some allegations as well after she was taken into custody. During the time my children were with me, they never said they were sexually abused. Now, I was faced with my daughter saying that the pastor had sexually touched her. Their lives and my life were spiraling out of control day after day.

I was alone. I was naked. I was humiliated. My self-righteous posture was broken down. How could this be my children, my church, my pastor, my life? God didn't love me anymore. I was abandoned. "I didn't do anything, so where are my children?" I questioned within myself.

I didn't know what I did wrong, and no one could tell me. The police officials, social workers and previous members of the church kept saying that the pastor is not who we thought he was. I kept hearing that from almost everyone outside of my church. How could I have lived a lie? I couldn't get over the fact that the child protective papers had my name on them. The police reports had my name on them. The court papers had my name on them. This is not what I was praying for all these years. Everything I worked for was now all gone.

It was embarrassing to face my mom, grandmother, sisters, and former classmates. I graduated in the top 10% of my high school class, I had received my bachelor's degree, I was just one semester from my master's degree; and I owned my own Christian school. I thought I was on my way to becoming a business owner and writing my first book on how great I was as an entrepreneur and mother of three children. Everything I hoped for was gone, and it seemed that my children were now my enemies. My children had not only sided with the girl in her allegations against the church, they also agreed with state officials that I had neglected them as their mother.

As I was watching my life flash in front of my eyes, it seemed that one minute I was a young girl chasing a dream and the next minute I was going to court for dependent neglect. The state was suing me for not protecting my children from the pastor who may have raped a young girl. He was not on trial for physical abuse, but sexual abuse. I never saw Pastor Menard sexually abuse anyone.

I could not grasp how he was the one being accused, and somehow, I was paying the price with him. Something went wrong here, very wrong. God, please help me!

Why didn't I just leave this church with my kids? All these thoughts went through my mind. There are several reasons. We were a family, and families will have arguments. Our pastor always used to say, "Families fight. You don't leave just because there are problems. You work through the problems." The ironic thing, however; was that the pastor was not talking about our biological families when he said this. This only applied to us in the church, not our biological families. It seemed that unless our biological families supported the church and the pastor, it was ok to have broken relationships with them.

Any family we had outside of the church was not considered our real family now that we were saved. That was the philosophy of our group. The way of thinking went something like this. The idea was that if there were problems in my church family, I needed to change my behavior and then there would be peace. Besides, God (as he was presented to me at age 19 years old) approved of this arrangement. It was I who needed to just learn to grow up and be stronger as a parent and follower. The pastor was the man of God, sent by God to look over my kids and me, and that meant that I had to stay.

Another reason I stayed with the church was I was spiritually born into this church at 19 years old. This was the only church I had ever known as an adult, so I had to stay. Where would I go? What pastor could counsel me? I didn't trust other pastors. My pastor would not allow us as his staff to visit churches on our own. We were only allowed to visit churches under the direction of our pastor only. Those times were few. We were taught that we were a special group. We thought we were an elite group when it came to other churches. We were taught the best Bible classes. In our opinion, our pastor was smarter than the other pastors in our circle, so I would be leaving a great teaching ministry and I couldn't risk being out of the elite group, so I had to stay.

I thought the pastor needed me. Whenever he had an outburst, he appeared humble and would say in a loving way that he just needed a vacation. Then he would explain that he felt like he continued to give his all to all of us, and very seldom did he ever take time for himself. He needed me to make sure he could get a vacation and said the other women and club members didn't understand his needs. He said his wife didn't understand him. He didn't have anybody to understand him but me, so I had to stay.

The luxuries of not having to pay my own bills or raising my kids alone or being without a support group would be gone if I left. I was terrified of the thought of raising my kids on my own. My ex-husband had his own new family, my mom did not understand me, and there were no other friends or relatives that would take me in.

My kids needed the firm hand of the pastor so that they would be successful in life. They were taught life skills while they were in Christian school. They were with me every day while I pursued my own college degree. The club staff helped care for my kids when I was in college classes at night. "Where would I be able to teach my kids those skills to this magnitude and still complete my degree at the same time?" I thought to myself.

The church club members supported me in my goal to save my kids from poverty, dropping out of high school, gang banging, drugs, and teen pregnancy, so I had to stay.

What about the homes, land, and church ministry that we (as a club family) were planning together? We all pledged to be lifetime members and sacrifice our money, time, and talents in order to build a comfortable life together. We were friends and business partners. We learned to suffer together, grow together, and laugh together. As long as the pastor remained respected and revered in our lives, we were okay. Well, I had to stay.

I thought I was doing what the Bible said by denying my mother, father, children and taking up my cross.

This was real for me.

These were the reasons I continued to stay with the church even while feeling like I was mentally exhausted and perplexed. I was willing to do whatever it took to keep my faithfulness to the church. There was one thing, however, that I was not willing to give up and that was my soul. After a while it felt like my life didn't belong to Jesus; it belonged to the pastor and the club. My life didn't even belong to the church; it belonged to the club. The club was taking my life, and to tell the truth, I was miserable inside.

In hindsight I now understand that all of these reasons were just excuses that I was telling myself. The truth was that I was afraid and embarrassed to tell anyone that something was wrong. I always felt like I was going to get in trouble for saying what I really felt about most issues. Again, I couldn't put my finger on what I was really feeling because I constantly had a struggle inside me: Is my life really what God wants for me? Or is this something else?

Although, I was sure he was the man of God, I felt like our pastor was unethical. He just didn't seem to view things like the average pastors I had heard about. In all of my inner turmoil regarding his methods of discipline and father-like interaction with me, I never thought he committed any crime against the children of our church and club. Absolutely not! He had inappropriate relationships with me and the other women, but (like he always said) we were consenting adults. I hated that part of my life more than the rest, but I lived with my decision.

Although I graduated from a four-year college with a bachelor's degree and was only one semester from graduating with my master's degree, I didn't believe I could make it on my own. Everyone in the club family repeatedly said to one another, "We could never make it on our own without the pastor." We constantly said that we all owed our success to him, especially me (because he helped me raise my kids), so I had to stay. As I reflected on the fact that our church was under investigation and my children were removed by the state, things were worse than ever I had experienced. This was the worst trial of my life!

Now something was happening that was changing my whole life. It was so intense, so surreal, so bizarre, that it taught me a life-long lesson. I couldn't believe what was happening. Everything I held dear to me was now crumbling down. My whole belief system was falling apart.

At the beginning of the investigation, the trial was about our pastor being accused of child rape of one of the girls in the church. As parents, we were all trying to grasp how outrageous this was and whether any of our own children were victims. Was our pastor guilty? Why would a child that we all loved make up such a horrible story? At first my daughter said nothing ever happened to her. My sons also said that they were never sexually abused. I believed that my kids were telling the truth when they said nothing sexual had ever happened to them.

However, I also knew that if the pastor did touch this girl, it would open a door for my kids to find a way out of the harsh discipline they received from the pastor over the years. Were my kids lying?

I started to believe that this whole investigation was not whether the pastor committed this crime or not, but whether this was the escape that the kids were looking for.

They felt they were physically abused and felt like there was no justice. I as their parent was physically abused and psychologically conditioned to accept the way things were. I minimized my abuse. Looking back on things, I can see that as a parent, I lived in continual fear of disobeying the rules and being emotionally punished. I, as a parent, was continually forced to change my point of view to blend in with the club's point of view. I no longer operated on mainstream thinking that said that parents were responsible for their own children's lives. I guess you could say I had already given up my parental rights as soon as I allowed the pastor to be that father figure in my life. The state really didn't have to do that - my parental rights were gone anyway.

I didn't believe that he would intentionally hurt any of my kids, and I still don't think that he would. Nonetheless, the hurt happened, and my daughter eventually disclosed that she was sexually molested. She said she was participating in sexual relations with the pastor.

Journal

Oh my God! I'm at a loss for words. This is not happening. NO, my daughter is not saying this. Is she? Somebody is making her say these things. How could this happen? He's the man of God!

At this time, I was a minister and assistant pastor who had a duty to stay with the church. I could stay or leave with my kids (who seemed to be lying on the pastor). To stay with the church meant that I would be denying my children, but I thought that to leave the church meant that I was denying God. What was God asking me to do?
I was confused. Is this whole thing a sick joke?

While I was standing in the empty sanctuary one day, through all my tears, I felt something leading me to a familiar Bible text. It was Psalms 91:1(KJV) which says, "He that dwelleth in the secret place of the most High shall abide under the shadow of the almighty…"

At that moment, it was clear to me that God was telling me to stay with the church and he would protect me. I wasn't sure what all of this meant, but it gave me some peace about my decision to stay although I longed to be with my kids. I felt like a horrible mother based on this decision, but to not follow it made me feel even worse. God was telling me to stay. Somehow, I knew that my staying was for a reason that I didn't understand yet. The most remarkable thing about this moment was that this was the first time I heard God speak to me without Pastor Menard! And I never told anyone until years later.

Meanwhile, hearing that my daughter was changing her testimony while in state custody was very distressing for me because for a long time she said nothing happened. But now after being coerced by police officers, she changed her mind and said she was molested. This is what I couldn't understand. In the same day, my daughter would tell me that nothing happened and then tell her brothers and social workers that something did happen. What was going on? She appeared to be living two different lives.

I lived in turmoil trying to decide when to believe her. Several years later, while she remained in state custody, I ended up believing my daughter when she said something did happened to her.

You see, it wasn't until later that I began to understand that my daughter was trying to protect me because I was still living with the club members. She never wanted to lose my love by telling me that she was molested. I was not able to handle the truth. Because I had decided to stay with the club and church, she understood that I would have been shunned while still living with the club members. To make sure I wouldn't be mistreated, she continued to recant her statements in order to protect me and ultimately his family too from the truth. She and the pastor's daughters were friends.

It seems that while our lives were torn apart, she was living in personal hell of her own. She had to choose between her mother's love and her own personal truth.

During those difficult 12 years, it was never clear what actually happened. In hindsight, I now understand that my daughter was trying to hold on to me by lying to me. She knew that our relationship would have ended if she told me the truth while I was still living with the club under their norms. I was still brainwashed, deeply rooted, and could not let go of the thought that it was God's will for me to be living with the only church family I had ever known. I was still addicted to the titles, influence, and power of being in this little club and church. Being with the church meant that I had growing influence within the other churches that were affiliated our church. I couldn't see then that I was putting my needs before my children.

My daughter and I knew that if she had told me the truth, I would be told by the pastor to disown her while he convinced me to turn my back on her and serve "God." Often, he would say that the children were lying on him. At that time, I believed that Pastor Menard would not lie, and I knew that my children would lie. I had learned long before this situation not to trust my kids. Our relationship was stripped of any mutual respect. We didn't even know how to talk to each other without the pastor being present.

My Kids are Gone!

I didn't know how to be anything but angry and outraged while my kids lived in state custody. As a result, I was rude to my kids and they were disrespectful to me. We had supervised visits while case managers stood around. I felt like I was treated as a criminal and the state was trying to keep my children away from me.

I was no longer allowed to make any of the decisions in their lives. They developed new friends and support systems without me. Whenever we saw each other, the conversations would end in anger, hurt, and emotional trauma on both sides. Back then, foster families and social workers told me when, where, and how long I could see my own children. My parental rights were still intact, but it didn't matter to social workers. Those rights were invisible.

And to make matters worse, I was forced to see my ex-husband after almost 15 years who showed up one day to take custody of the kids. It was humiliating on all levels. Family members came in and rescued my children so that they did not have to stay in state custody very long, but every night that they were in foster homes, terror seized my heart. All I could think about was whether I was going to get a call from the state informing me that something had happened to my kids while in the state's care. I heard so many horror stories about kids getting lost in the system, being abused, or coming up dead. My worst nightmare had just taken place by having them as wards of the state and me being pegged as a bad mother.

Reflecting on the whole process, I can still feel the emotional suffering of having my children removed from my home. The pain was beyond words. Before they were taken, I agreed with the demands of the Child Protection workers to not attend church anymore and to keep my children at home away from Pastor Menard, but they were still removed. That devastating blow sent me into a whirlwind of depression and confusion. Each day I realized that I would no longer be a part of their lives- no high school graduation, no proms. I would be missing all of their other achievements. We were no longer a family. We were enemies. I couldn't see how this whole thing was an answer to my prayer. This is not what I prayed, Lord!

This was not what I prayed for at all, or was it? There were some pretty miraculous things that happened during the trial that made me wonder just how much God was behind all of this. Was it a blessing in disguise? Although I lost my home, business, church, my children and the respect of peers I went to school with, I never lost my mind, my hope, and will to serve God. To be honest, all of this could have caused me to turn away from God altogether, but the opposite happened. I moved toward God like never before; expecting that a loving God would help me.

Through this I learned so much about God. The first lesson was that there was only one true God, and Pastor Menard was not it. I was not it. And the only true God was sovereign. That blew my mind! God protected my children when they went into state custody and as they continued their lives. My mom was with me in court the very next day when the judge took my kids. She gave me money to get an attorney and continued to show love towards me throughout the whole time I was living this lie. She knew that something was wrong for years and tried on many occasions to tell me to get out. I would not listen, and I even cursed her out in a religious way. I put her down bad, but her love continued. She did all she could to help my children until I was ready for repentance. My mother in law stepped in to take care of my children's education and gave them a place to stay that was safe. Because of her sacrifice, my sons graduated with college degrees and now own their own businesses.

To this day she is still paying student loans for them. Their grandmothers stepped up to the plate and sacrificed to help all my children. I didn't know it then, but now I know that my daughter had a wonderful foster mom that made sure my daughter was safe while she struggled to finish high school at night. My daughter suffered so much from the lifestyle she endured while in my care, but today she is completing her college degree while raising her own children. She's a survivor. There were so many others who guided my kids to wholeness; their hearts were in it. God touched their hearts. I know this was a rare blessing because nowadays there are very few grandparents and strangers in this world that will help others under such dire circumstances.

The Light at the End of the Tunnel

The investigation lasted for approximately three long years.
After the trial I really saw the light. Pastor Menard was not convicted, no evidence was found. None of the families were charged with anything, no evidence was found. Some of the families received their children back, but my children never came back.

Even though the results of the trial seemed to be favorable, my children did not come back to me. During the three years they remained in state custody and eventually moved to another state with their other family members on their father's side. The next 12 years, I was on my own. I did not have the responsibility or fear of raising my kids anymore. I began to feel that I didn't need the pastor as active in my life because I was now a single person with no kids. In hindsight, this seems to have been the best opportunity for God to get my attention.

During those years without my kids, I cried almost every day, but I had time to reflect on my life and really pay attention to why I made the choices I did.

Through introspection, I discovered who the real culprit was that caused me to make the decisions I made. His name is fear. Fear had been my bosom buddy ever since I was a child, and now I began to seriously question why it had so much power in my life.

During those 12 years, God began to slowly reveal the private evidence that I needed in looking at what just happened in my life. And oh, my God, something was not right in the club camp!

There is really something magical about the Scripture that teaches that we should be quick to listen and slow to speak. During these 12 years, I learned just that.

As I stopped participating in all of the church events and meetings, I began to just watch things and listen to the conversations around me. I didn't know what I was looking for. I just felt like I needed to relinquish all my titles and get back to the basics of my salvation and relationship with God. Pastor Menard and I grew apart, and I was feeling some relief and peace with that.

In the meantime, having the traumatic interference of state officials lurking in the corners of our every action, paranoia was a feeling that was a battle for me for a little while. Are they coming to handcuff me? Are they planning to come back and take whatever dignity was left in me? It was a nightmare. But as time went on, something beautiful did take place. I began to reach out to my biological family members in a new way. Still filled with self-righteousness and anger, I managed to have moments of clarity. At these times, I realized more and more just what was really important in my life. I discovered that I really appreciated the friendships and good times with my club family, but I constantly longed for my biological family more. I also longed for truth and love. More and more, I just wanted to be free from the lifestyle I was in. Every chance I got, I visited home to see my biological family more often. Every year I took vacation time to be with them and get away. Sometimes I felt guilty for leaving the church and club members, but it's what I had to do in order to clear my mind.

It was the wisdom of my aunt, who was once a voice of reason for me as a child, that told me one day to stop, shut up, and listen. She said in a very gentle voice, "Just stop. Stop talking in your life. Be quiet and start listening to the things around you." It was that simple.

It was clear what she meant. By having all the titles, promotions and busy-work in the church, all these years I spent too much time giving my opinion, joining every committee, and working to please man. And now it was time to just STOP. I stopped being involved in every discussion, activity, or event in the church or club. The truth is I was mentally exhausted and not able to just turn back to a normal life. I was withdrawn most times. Through all of this, I was able to watch the behavior of the pastor, the state of the church ministry and the club members. I even watched my own behavior for next few years. Holding on to my memory of being alone with God in the sanctuary that day, I began to put the pieces of my life back together. I also started noticing things that I had never realized before.

To my surprise, I learned there was something else present with us other than God. Notice I said other than God. This implies that God was there in our lives. He was there, and through each difficult step in putting my life back together, I could sense His presence. Slowly I learned to sit in his presence when no one else was looking. It was private.

Also, being in a small town, something like this drew a lot of attention, and there were many nights where I was too embarrassed to just go to Walmart because of the all the bad publicity. I stopped leaving the house except for absolutely, necessary errands and appointments. I guess you could say I learned to be still. The church was torn apart and the only ones that remained were the club members.

In all of this, God had a way of talking to me when no one else was talking. For the span of the next 12 years, God kept talking to me about this incident until I finally woke up! After I spiritually and emotionally woke up, you wouldn't believe what happened next. Evil was living among us. I've come to believe that…

Evil is not simply the absence of good.

Evil is 99% good and 1% evil.

Chapter 6
Summary

Painfully, as I was writing this book, I experienced repeated mental and physical attacks on my body. I believe these attacks happened so that my testimony would not make it to these pages. Attacked? Yes, attacked.

Who attacked me? It was by the enemy of Christ, Satan, and he did it through the form of witchcraft.

The attacks I experienced while writing this are connected to the series of the events that began in West Germany some 30 years ago. In retrospect, I believe that God allowed me to endure witchcraft and spiritual abuse in order to help others. I lived through it so that I could tell you about it. Witchcraft is real. And God plans to set people free from this satanic abuse. He will rescue His people and my testimony is just a glimpse of what He can do.

What About Witchcraft?

It seems that many people don't believe in witchcraft, but it has been my experience that teenagers and young adults are fully aware of it. It's the religious generation that seems to deny its existence by simply ignoring it altogether, or if they are aware, by trying to defeat it with lukewarm tactics. When I say religious, I am talking about those who half-heartedly give their time and money to God with no real commitment or very little concern about how He views their lives. They are lukewarm, living their religious lives being their own judges rather than adhering to and obeying the voice of God. These are those who go to church but regularly live in the flesh while joking about it and thinking it's ok. They assume that being materially blessed means that God is pleased with their lives. We forget that God's goodness rains on the just as well as the unjust.

Let me tell you, being materially blessed is not a good way to tell if God is pleased with you. Neither is being poor. Some believe that living like a pauper makes you somehow closer to God, and that's just not so. Likewise, having a large church and driving a fancy car does not make you more holy either. God is pleased with us when we allow His will to become our will. He is pleased when we live our lives in submission to the leading and guiding of His spirit. Our righteousness is as filthy rags in His sight. The way to know that God is really pleased with us is by how often we submit to His will and not our own. We can have pleasures and good things happen for us while still living in disobedience to God's will. If we are Christians, living in disobedience to God and being content with that is living a lukewarm life. As Christians we are not perfect, but we should be concerned about whether our lives and actions are in accordance to God's will every day. It matters! And the Scripture teaches that those who are content with being lukewarm in their walk with Christ are prime candidates for the works of the flesh to breed in their lives.

Galatians 5:19 says, "When you follow the desires of your sinful nature, the results are very clear: sexual immorality, impurity, lustful pleasures, idolatry, sorcery …" (NLT, Life Recovery Bible)

As seen in Scripture, when we walk in the flesh, we allow other sins to enter in our lives, sometimes unaware. Witchcraft (sorcery) is one of these sins, although there are many other types of works of the flesh (sins) that enter in as well. Galatians 5 lists several types, but the one that seems to get overlooked a lot is witchcraft. Today, witchcraft in the church is more common than we think. Many are either using witchcraft (whether knowingly or not) and others are being attacked by witchcraft (whether knowingly or not). Yes, there are witches in God's church, and there are also those who aid in witchcraft through ignorance. Despite how it is being done, witchcraft is practiced more than we think. And many of us are being affected by it each day unaware.

The word sorcery is another name for witchcraft which is *pharmakeia* in the Greek language, and it refers to *magic*, and in some cases *medication* that is given by a poisoner.

According to the Bible, a witch is one who practices magic or whispers spells. That is their "craft" or job.

If you are attacked by witchcraft, it cannot be "praised away," and neither can it be "churched away." Having more church does not get rid of witchcraft. The Bible teaches that the weapons against witchcraft and other demonic forces come from total surrender and submission to God, and after that, the regular application of His word. There are so many religious people who try to fight spiritual things half-heartedly, without total submission to Christ. Other people just prefer not to talk about it even though there is more and more evidence in our society supporting that witchcraft does really exist. In any case, witchcraft is on the rise because it is not being recognized and properly handled by those who claim to know Christ. Unfortunately, I was one of these people who did not recognize witchcraft some years ago. Witchcraft used to wreak havoc on my life because I was not aware of it. Now, I am able to recognize it and resist it with the help of the Lord.

If you are a teenager or young person reading this book, it's possible that a lot of things that I revealed may not have been a surprise to you. I guess the real surprise is that witchcraft is still widespread in our churches and families even though Christians claim to have power over it.

Let's be clear, we, as believers DO have power over ALL the power of the enemy (Luke 10:19). The problem is that if we walk in the flesh, we allow the enemy an entrance into our lives. Witchcraft, then, can cause continued terror in our lives because we are not following God's leading. On the other hand, if we are walking in the spirit of God and doing God's will, we may sometimes be attacked by the enemy through witchcraft. In that case, we will be armed and ready in God's spirit to oppose or "resist" the devil. The only way to resist the devil as a Christian is through total submission to God. Walking in the spirit of God is walking in submission to God's word and His will in our lives.

To a person who is walking in the flesh and living in disobedience to God's will, you are powerless to these attacks and engaging in an unauthorized battle with Satan.

To the person walking in the spirit of God and obeying His will, these attacks can be overcome and stopped through your faith and the power of Jesus Christ, our savior.

Somehow many of us in the church who claim to know the power of God have been ill-prepared in protecting ourselves and our families from attacks of the enemy, and so witchcraft and other sins continue right in our homes and churches undetected and unhandled.

To be straight about it, witchcraft is not going to stop; it's gonna get worse. Witchcraft will get worse because we (who refuse to acknowledge it) will give it room to grow. Just like roaches multiply because we either ignore the few we see or we use the wrong pesticides to kill them, witchcraft is growing all around us.

Most people know that roaches can infest and take over our homes if we do not stop them. This is what is happening with witchcraft and demonic attacks. The Bible teaches that as Christians, we will be persecuted, there will be attacks.

However, it has been my experience that there are spiritual attacks wreaking havoc on our lives unnecessarily. God did not ordain all of these attacks. The question is why then are they happening? While writing this book, I was being attacked in my dreams, I was attacked sometimes through mental exhaustion, and even attacked with sudden illnesses or unexplained pains in my body. Although unpleasant, I understood the reasons. It was because the enemy was trying to stop this writing. The important thing here is that when I prayed and was obedient through this journey, these attacks stopped, and I recovered each time.

I'm glad to say that although persecution will come, so will the peace of God.

Witchcraft has been around since the beginning of time, and it will continue to spread and affect our lives until something is done. It is sin in the sight of God, and unfortunately, it lives in God's house like roaches. And it's time to do something about it.

How do you know if you're being attacked?

The most direct way that I can answer this question is by saying this: God will let you know whether you are being attacked by some form of witchcraft. Many times, we do not know we are being persecuted by witchcraft. We all must follow the leading of the Holy Spirit.

Furthermore, in any environment that allows blatant disobedience to God's commands, there is room for works of the flesh to emerge. This can happen in businesses, social groups, organizations, governments, nations, families, personal lives, and even in churches.

Usually starting with feelings of confusion, witchcraft attacks drain strength and energy. Fatigue is often experienced during a witchcraft attack. Witchcraft attacks drain the life right out of you. When attacked, you feel tired, depressed, oppressed, and fatigued. You can take vitamins, exercise, run five miles, and it still doesn't help.

Others feel sad, sleep all the time, feel trapped in depression and can't get out.

It is the spiritual force that Christians feel when under demonic attack. These kinds of spiritual attacks are identified like great confusion, wanting to give up and quit, and depression. ("Spiritual Discernment and Prayer Against Witchcraft Attacks," www.jonasclark.com)

Why am I talking so much about witchcraft? It's because so many Christians are under these spiritual attacks, and it's time to be free. Just remember, this is not new information. These attacks are active today and have been active for years. Only by God's grace, this writing was not stopped by these attacks.

What Happened to Me Years Ago?...

Well, I began experiencing weird things after I joined a church in Germany in 1986. There were strange things happening to me, my husband and my three children all while we were there, but I just kept dismissing them. I kept thinking that it was all in my mind. Instead of leaving the church, we stayed; after three years, I and my three children ended up attending the same church when it moved to the United States. I can't explain why, but I was so into this church that I packed up my three children who were babies at the time and I left my husband in Germany to rejoin the church in the United States. It was like I was addicted to something in this church.

There was something that kept drawing me to this church even though many times I just felt like my life was getting worse and worse. It seemed as though my attitude about life, my family, and God was changing in weird ways, and I could not stop it. Something was happening in this church, but I just could not put my finger on it. At first, I thought it was good, but honestly there were times where I was totally confused. In hindsight, I now believe that there was spiritual abuse happening. Spiritual abuse is a fairly new term for me. I really didn't know how to describe what I experienced until I ran across this word once I left the church some 20 years later.

Spiritual abuse refers to a church elder or faith leader inflicting abuse on congregation members, often by creating a toxic culture within the church or group by shaming or controlling members using the power of their position. However, spiritual abuse can also occur within an intimate partner relationship.

Spiritual abuse is not limited to a certain religion or denomination. Any person, of any belief system, is capable of perpetrating spiritual abuse, just as anyone can be the victim of it. (National Domestic Violence Hotline, www.thehotline.org)

A common characteristic of an abusive religious system is that the real needs of the people are lost in the never-ending quest by the leaders for personal fulfillment and happiness. (Warning Signs of Spiritual Abuse 2018 The Christian Broadcasting Network, Inc., A nonprofit 501 (c)(3) Charitable Organization).

I'm a Christian, and I do not believe that ALL Christian churches are allowing abuse in their congregations, but I do believe there is a system of spiritual abuse that is happening more often than we think and its right under our noses. It's much bigger than us.

You see, what happened to me and my family in the church could happen anywhere. Spiritual abuse and witchcraft are exercised through the control of another's will. When spiritual abuse is allowed in church, many times witchcraft is present as well. As a matter of fact, I have seen the same witchcraft that was in the church also happening in the schools that many of our children are attending, and it's happening even in the homes of our kids' classmates. I'll talk more about what's happening with our youth in another book. Nonetheless, witchcraft and spiritual abuse are common in many arenas.

Witchcraft is carried out in movies and in certain types of music that we listen to. Oh, but I don't have to tell you that. Some of you already know. If you are being attacked by witchcraft now through a toxic relationship, I'm here to tell you that God has a plan to bring you out of that situation. He is calling you away from churches that are spiritually abusive and that are putting you to sleep through demonic tactics. Toxic churches put you to sleep so that satanic forces can destroy your life. You see, a lot of God's people in the church are being spiritually and psychologically raped/blinded on many levels by witchcraft and other satanic works. That's why darkness moves so freely within their lives.

Because so many Christians are spiritually asleep, only a few are listening to the warnings. God is speaking to them, to me and to you, but a lot of God's people are just not listening!

He is saying: WAKE UP! You Gotta' WAKE UP, and WAKE UP, NOW!

To find out what happened the next 12 years, check out, "Stop! He Will Find You," part II.

Jesus Will Find you,
No matter how weird,
No matter how lonely
No matter how crazy,
No matter how queer,
No matter how far,
No matter how deep,
No matter how long,
No matter how steep,
No matter how dry,
No matter how strong,
No matter how scary,
No matter how wrong,
Jesus will find you
And bring you home

-by T.M. White

A Note from me (the author) to YOU...

We all have a story. And like me, you have your own story that needs to be told. In 2014, after my 28 year ordeal, my mom (who passed away before this publication) encouraged me with these words:

"The life you lived was your journey to Christ. Everyone has a journey to Christ. Don't look down on yours."

Don't' look down on your journey.

Your sister in the faith,

Tonya

In loving memory of my mom, Saundra M. Humphrey

T. Dailey, author of the "Stop, He Will Find You: A Personal Testimony of Bondage and Deliverance" series, has devoted herself to telling the truth about what really happens when you become lured into a religious cult through ignorance and arrogance. Making a decision that sent her family into almost thirty years of spiritual torment and abuse, her testimony reveals how God's love can pull families, loved ones and anyone from the depths of satanic bondage and from some of the most misfortunate situations where trust should have been the last thing questioned.

She was born to Tom E. White and Saundra M. Humphrey on the south Side of Chicago, Illinois in 1967. At the young age of 18 years old, she met her husband who decided to serve in the United States Military. After high school graduation, T. Dailey was blessed to give birth to their first child, a baby girl. As military dependents, T. Dailey and her new family moved to West Germany to live for approximately three years. While there, T. Dailey conceived again and birthed a set of identical twin boys.

Suddenly, she found herself being a wife and mom of three children all by the young age of 20 years old. Life had moved very quickly, and she was keeping up with it. Playing many roles for everyone around her was an important part of life.

While still at this tender age, she made the bold decision to serve in the Christian ministry. She would go on to dedicate many years to serving as a Christian minister still unaware of the underlying spiritual abuse surrounding her.

During her time being a mother and devoted Christian, she had a profound encounter with Christ that forever shaped the rest of her life. And despite insurmountable challenges, her devotion has never wavered.

Because she still held education at a high place, T. Dailey obtained her Master of Science Degree in Human Services and Leadership Development from Murray State University in Murray, Kentucky. This, coupled with her newfound relationship with Christ, helped to flourish the things she valued most.

Now, she is a newly established writer, and has spent over 10 years as a social worker and educational coach to families and youth (K-12). She is founder and CEO of S.T.I.L.L. Ministries, a non- profit organization that supports women who are healing from the effects of spiritual abuse.

As the author of, "Stop, He Will Find You: A Personal Testimony of Spiritual Bondage" part1 and 2, she continues to share her testimonies with the world. T. Dailey is currently completing her next book, part 2 of the "Stop, He Will Find You" series while establishing a homeschool business to help families with 7 th -12 th grade students. She lives in the state of Wisconsin with her loving husband, children and grandchildren.

www.ingramcontent.com/pod-product-compliance
Lightning Source LLC
Chambersburg PA
CBHW061800070526
44586CB00023B/2654